Anna Barbara and Anthony Perliss

Invisible
Architecture

Experiencing Places through the Sense of Smell

SKIRA

Cover
Solitary Confinement, D Block, Alcatraz Prison,
San Francisco Bay (detail)
photo by A. Perliss, 2004

Design and layout
Irene Poma

Editorial Coordination
Giovanna Rocchi

Editing
Michele Abate

Translations
Robert Burns, Language Consulting Congressi, Milan

First published in Italy in 2006 by
Skira Editore S.p.A.
Palazzo Casati Stampa
via Torino 61
20123 Milano
Italy
www.skira.net

Printed and bound in Italy. First edition

ISBN-13: 978-88-7624-267-0
ISBN-10: 88-7624-267-8

Distributed in North America by Rizzoli International Publications, Inc.,
300 Park Avenue South, New York, NY 10010.
Distributed elsewhere in the world by Thames and Hudson Ltd., 181a High Holborn,
London WC1V 7QX, United Kingdom.

ACKNOWLEDGEMENTS

This book has been made possible thanks to the generosity, support, passion, curiosity, and love of many people.

THANKS TO Roger Schmid for our initiation into the world of odors; to Luca Molinari for his faith in us; to Irene Poma for everything; to the Università dell'Immagine with its plethora of extraordinary individuals who have contributed directly or indirectly to this book, but also to entire chapters of our respective lives. Hence, special thanks to Tania Gianesin, Maria Sebregondi, Paola Goretti, Nancy Martin, Benedetta Barzini, Fabrizio Ferri, David Bychkov, Letizia Schmid, Sara Manazza, Raphael Monzini, Romina Savi, Erminia De Luca, Nicola Pozzani, Isaac Sinclair, and also to Anna Piovesan, Carolina Pineiro, Nekane Leorza, Sara Pittaluga, Alessandro Boccingher, Marta & Bernat, Luis Blanco, Laura Mega, Francesca Ripamonti, and all the exceptional kids who would fill an endless list, and very special thanks to Carolina Rapetti with her lucid mind and steadfast heart encouraging, supporting, and brightening the most broad-ranging pathways of creativity.

THANKS TO Fabrizio Gallanti for his Chilean flowers, to Benedetta Mucchi, to Gianni Pezzani, to Alberto Rebori, fellow student and close friend, to Ida Farè, to Gisella Bassanini and Sandra Bonfiglioli for their encouragement; to Luc Gwiadzinski for having suggested the night.

THANKS TO Martin & Françoise Gras, Petra Blaisse, Pieter Keune from *De Kat Windmill*, Dick Husslage, Elizabeth Diller, Olympia Kazi, Maurice Roucel, Philippe Rahm, Lorenzo Villoresi, Clino Trini Castelli, Paolo Luzzi of the Botanical Gardens, Jean-Claude Ellena, Hervé Ellena, Olivier Monteil, and Anne Rebesche.

THANKS TO Antonio Petrillo who is no longer with us but who sparked many of the thoughts we have developed in this book.

THANKS TO all my students, who are greater sources of inspiration and beacons of thought and reasoning than they imagine. May they learn to use their noses, to connect their brains and their hearts; and to design.

THANKS TO Herbert, Cheryl, Sarah and Tessa, to Tina, Franco, Gigi, Salva, Maria, Giusy, Marco, Bettina, Andrea, Ninni, Flavia, Ornella, and Dario.

But above all, thanks to Enrico for his steadfast passion and to Naikari for her gentle determination.

TO MARGHERITA, THE NAME OF A SCENTED FLOWER, A DAISY AND A DELICIOUS DAUGHTER,

AND TO ROCCO WHO SPRAYS MY PERFUME ON HIS SISTER'S DOLLS,

TO ANNALISA, ELENA, CICCIO, ANDREA, ALEXIA, VANESSA, STELLA, THE QUINN TWINS, LEILA AND HENRY, LUCY, EVA, COLETTE, YUN TIAN, VITO, ANGIOLINO, FRANCESCO, PIETRO, FLORA, LUCIA, LORENZO, GABRIELE, MATILDE, SIMONE, LORENZO ROSSO, FILIPPO, BIANCA, GIUDITTA, AGATA, MATILDE GRANDE, GIULIA, SOFIA, CARLO, ANNINA, LUIGI, MARTA, CHECCO, LEILA, CECILIA, OLIVIA, EDWARD JOHN, JACOPO, ROSSELLA, LEONARDO, RUBEN, MARTA C., ELEONORA C., LORENZA, REBECCA, CATERINA, ELEONORA, IRENE, DARIO, DAVID, LUKAS, LISA, GIULIA PICCOLA, EMMA, TERESA, AND THE SURVIVING CHILDREN OF THE BESLAN SCHOOL,

TO THE TINY BEING IN SARA'S WOMB

AND TO ALL THE OTHER CHILDREN AROUND US SO THAT THEY MAY LEARN TO SMELL THE ODORS OF THE WORLD,

TO RECOGNIZE THEM AND INVENT NEW ONES.

PREFACE
10
INTRODUC
13
BIBLIOGRA
216
CONTRIBU
218
INDEX
219

1 CHAPTER
MORTE ED ENTROPIA
16
The Last Breath
18
Separate the Dwelling
Place of the Dead from
Those of the Living
18
The Nose of Architecture
19
The Architecture of the
Nose
22
Alchemy and Pharmacy
24
Putrescine and Cadaverine
25
Humors *by Sara Manazza*
26
Dosages and
Concentrations
28
Scatology
29
Futurism and Necrophilia
31
Blood
32
Punishment
35
Food
36
Eau de New Orleans
37
Volatile Organic Compounds
38
Dust
40
Odorless Death
41
The Catacombs, Paris:
Philippe Rahm and
Maurice Roucel
45

2 CHAPTER
EMOTIONS AND
RITES
50
Architecture as Urns
53
Odor of Sanctity
54
Earthly Paradise and
Heavenly Garden
55
Gardens
56
21 grams
by Romina Savi
58
Secrets
59
Sulfur
60
The Place of Fire
61
Per fumum
64
Listening to Incense
65
Tobacco
67
The Tea Ceremony and
Coffee Rituals
68

3 CHAPTER
MARKETING AND
TME
72
Conservation and
Acceleration
74
Greenhouses
76
A tour of Parma, City
of Perfume
by Nicola Pozzani
78
The Genie of the Lamp
79
Vacuum Packed
80
The Medium is the
Message
81
Travel and Trade
85
Physiological Architecture
86
Subliminal
87
Air Pandang
by Nancy Martin
89
Emotional Marketing
90
Removal
92
Placebo
93
Les ateliers Hermès, Paris:
Hervé Ellena and Jean-
Claude Ellena
97

4

CHAPTER
IDENTITY AND
MEMORY
104
"To smell"
106
Non-Standard Architectures
107
Being-Essence
109
Circuits and Connections
111
Absence-Essence
by Carolina Rapetti
112
Words
114
The evaporating subject
by Letizia Schmid
116
Olfactory Material
117
Compositions
118
Vernacular, Tribal, Hypogeal
120
Memory
122
Mediterranean
124
City Odors
125
Undiclosed Recipient
by Fabrizio Gallanti
126
Open 24 Hours
128
*The Meatpacking District,
New York York:
Elizabeth Diller and
Roger Schmid*
133

5

CHAPTER
BODIES AND
DISTANCES
138
Territory and Belonging
140
The Trigeminus and the
Olfactory Compass
141
Animality
142
Pet me
144
Sports
146
Attraction and Repulsion
147
Seduction
149
Sexuality
150
Anthropology
152
George Orwell
153
Fresh Air Break
156
Atmosphere is My Style
157
*The Zaanse Windmills,
Amsterdam: Petra Blaisse
And Martin Gras*
161

6

CHAPTER
DRY OR $\frac{1}{2}$UMID
168
Epidemics
170
Erasmus and the Birth of
Manners
171
Morality
172
Utopias and Hygiene
173
The Bourgeois Home
174
Dry Century
177
Vapors and Fogs
178
Spas, Baths, and Saunas
181
Natural and Forced-Air
Ventilation: the Beginnings
183
The Wind Rose
184
*Giardino dei Semplici,
Florence: Lorenzo Villoresi
and Clino Trini Castelli*
189

7

CHAPTE
REALTY AND
REPRODUCTIONS
196
Reaffirming the Real
198
Vanilla and Vanillin
200
Eating Aromas
201
The beauty of nature and
its vast diversity lies in its
simplicity
by Isaac Sinclair
202
Hallucinatory States and
Meta-spaces
203
Sometimes They Come
Back Again: Odorama and
Synesthesia
205
Symbiotic Fragrance and
the Rise of Meta-Humanity
by Raphael Monzini
206
Ubiquity
208
Hyperventilation
209
PIANODORANT: a Dream
Instrument
by David Bychkov
210
Symbiotic Fragrance and
the Rise of Meta-Humanity
212

Preface

JOSEPH RYKWERT RELATES THAT WHEN ONE OF HIS STUDENTS MENTIONS, for example, types of Greek architecture, Rykwert would ask what the Greeks were doing in the building. What was happening, for instance, on the altar? This was where cows, bulls, and other animals were slaughtered in sacrifice. So there was blood and stench… We never think about these things, but they are an important part of our consciousness of a building.

This book started as series of questions that we authors have asked ourselves in different circumstances when confronted with the variegated world of odors. Our different paths have led us to wonder how to represent, in a visual culture, the sense of smell and its attributes and how to use it as a tool in the architectural design process.

One question sparked another and we have sought to address them all in this book: why aren't odors – beyond fragrances, perfumes, candles or incense – used as ingredients in the design process? Why is the olfactory dimension almost never explored by those outside of the world of perfume and chemistry? What is the architecture of olfactory structures?

This book began to take form around questions such as these. Over the years it has become a bona fide journey through the history and geography of places that have a meaningful relationship with smells, air, and olfaction. This journey has made us aware that there are many places that can only be fully explored by following invisible olfactory traces, that the related issues are of cardinal importance, and that there are a number of surprising connections between olfaction and architecture.

We deliberately did not limit our investigation to pleasant scents and aromas, but cast a broader net that embraced everything from the foulest stenches to the most sublime perfumes, from the conscious use of air as a resource to its ability to function as a time machine. We looked into both the physiological characteristics and the organoleptic qualities associated with the sense of smell. The result is a collection of notes and thoughts on the incredible interplay between certain places and odors. It has helped us approach otherwise incomprehensible issues and opened up pathways begging further exploration. We have indicated places encountered along the way of only one of the possible paths, which will give an idea of just how much there still is to explore.

Our research has led us to the realization that, in spite of their apparent differences, there are compelling points of contact between perfumers and architects. In many ways they share a similar language and address similar issues. And so we decided to bring these two professions together in conversation, inviting them to challenge one another on certain issues. No one declined the invitation and this provided further encouragement to us to continue.

The meeting places were never random, but always in some way linked to the world of odors: the catacombs of Paris; the Zaansdrake windmills in Holland; the Meatpacking district in New York; the Giardino dei Semplici in Florence; the Hermès leatherworking atelier in Paris.

Along with these specialists we met with people in other disciplines who were also exploring issues related to the sense of smell. They have provided food for thought and insights that indicate new directions to take in exploring the territory. We also have sought to suggest, via the visual media available to publishers, the olfactory sensations of the selected locales.

Getting involved in the world of odors in a somewhat "heretical" way, i.e., not via the rigorous discipline of perfumery school or "nose training", has left us free to explore and interrelate in a cross-disciplinary manner topics and people that otherwise might have remained confined to specialized fields.

While the experts might see this work as going over well-traveled ground, we hope it will arouse the curiosity of those who are less well schooled in issues of the nose. It is to this latter group that this book is addressed.

It has been a delightful journey that has given us the sensation of moving, a bit like pioneers, into uncharted areas, into spaces to be discovered, explored, and inhabited. We could have gone on forever, but like all real-world journeys, we eventually reach a point of arrival, where we stop, unload, and share what we have gathered.

Introduction

THE TITLE, *INVISIBLE ARCHITECTURE. EXPERIENCING PLACES THROUGH THE SENSE OF SMELL*, reminds us that olfactory structures are mainly invisible even if they are almost always active and meaningful in the way we experience a place. But it is also a reference to an exhibition by Philippe Rahm and Jean-Gilles Décosterd, titled *Architecture invisible*, which aptly reflects many of the topics explored.

Western culture has been historically focused more on sight than on the other senses and is reluctant to consider other dimensions that nevertheless are fundamental in the experience of architecture, design, and habitation. Here olfaction would seem to be mostly extraneous to the formulation of spaces, and yet a careful reading of cognitive, perceptive, cultural, social, planning, and anthropological phenomena would seem to indicate that odors are not only profoundly inherent components of places, but at times are actually essential to defining them.

Richard Neutra commented in 1949 that we should devote as much attention as possible to all the non-visual aspects of our environment. He thus anticipated the design limits of those who fail to consider the other senses. It is a surprising affirmation because it dates from a time when we never would have suspected such issues to surface, when the dictates of Modernism were in full swing and the dominance of the visual dimension had yet to be challenged. Yet Neutra, working on architecture at the edges of the desert, could not limit himself to formal functionalism while the fine and pungent earth around him filled his eyes and nostrils.

There are innumerable reasons for this lack of regard for the sense of smell in architecture. We will explore some of them in this book.

A very evident issue simply lies in the invisible nature of the olfactory experience, which can hardly be addressed using the usual vision-based tools of design. In order to be considered, the invisible often has to invent other

Smells like Art by
Surasi Kusolwong,
Bangkok (photo by
A. Barbara, 2000)

13

media, formulate new expressive languages, become clear and evident – in other words, make itself visible – or risk oblivion.

Another reason is found in the intimate relation between smells and emotion. Olfaction is a profound perceptive sphere that can stir primal and at times ungovernable emotions in people generally and in designers specifically. The evocative potential of the sense of smell derives from the power of emotions. Odor is a powerful vehicle for memory and as such penetrates into our deepest recollections evoking the emotions that a given scent had originally stimulated, bringing back to the surface pleasures or pains that invariably stir our feelings anew.

And again, the sense of smell is extremely evanescent and intangible, caught up in the dynamic flow of time like sound and natural light. And because of this evanescence it is ungovernable in Western design culture with its roots in Greek culture, centered around sight, hearing, and touch. However, precisely because of its intangibility and transcendence, olfaction is deeply embedded in the foundations of oriental culture.

The thought of retracing a possible history of odors in architecture means recognizing almost immediately not only the cultural differences between East and West, but also between North and South, between the various regions of the world, between xeric and swampy land, between tropical climates and arid zones, between alpine huts and underground lairs, between local specificity and global homogeneity.

The relationship between space and odor is influenced by a complex of odors: those of the materials creating the space, of the furnishings within it, and the activities occurring in the space over the course of time. It also depends on the orientation of the space, the humidity of the air, and the persistence, saturation, timing, and nature of the odors. *In sum*, it is the result of a plethora of elements that are extremely difficult, if not impossible, to account for.

Nevertheless, if we want to address the issue of odors in architecture we cannot get around the questions that Tala Klinck poses in the book *Immaterial/Ultramaterial* edited by Toshiko Mori. She wants to know how polished marble, urethane-coated wood, and hot laminated steel smell in the buildings of Alvaro Siza. She wonders how the resins, solvents, and pigments contained in latex paints, drywall, nylon carpets, or epoxy carpet glues influence our perception of the spaces. Rudolph e-Khoury asserts that the modern surface is the extension of a visual logic of cleanliness and that the universal appeal of the white wall in modern architecture derives from its capacity to translate the absence of odor into an image. Klinck sees all this as a historic turning point.

This is perhaps the strongest sensation that our research for this book has left us with: the feeling that we are at a "historic turning point" in studies on the sense of smell. This feeling is supported by the awarding of the Nobel Prize for Medicine in 2004 to Richard Axel and Linda Buck for their work in clarifying the mechanisms that control the way in which odors are perceived at the molecular and the cellular levels. And we are left with the feeling that this invisible dimension of architecture is increasingly immanent, becoming material for study and research, and of artistic and architectural design, as never before.

DEATH/
ENTROPY

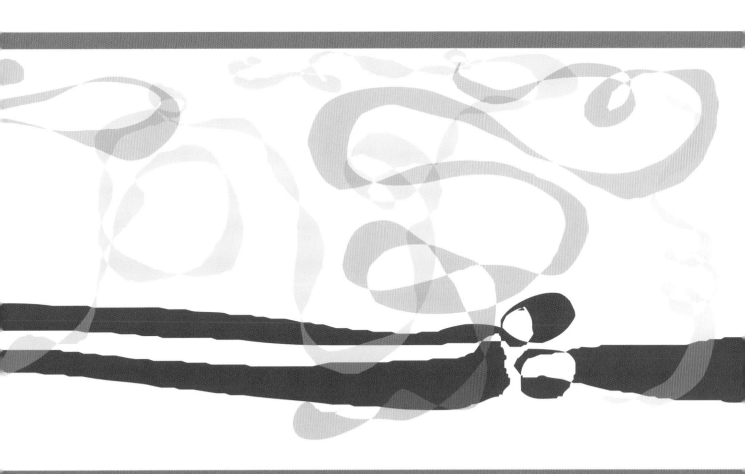

The Last Breath

The relation of the physical and metaphysical body with death and entropy is one of the most important keys to understanding the relationship of odors with the here and now, with earthly life and the things of this world. Death is an experience strongly associated with odors, of the physical body that separates from the spiritual body. The former decomposes and returns to the earth, the other volatilizes, exhaling a "last breath" that is the vehicle for the exit from the material and the change of state.

Death has always been associated with perfumed or mephitic exhalations depending on the specific cases, contexts, and even the biographies of the deceased. As a consequence, the rites and places of death have always been odorous, impregnated with an olfactory dimension that is the true narration of this passage.

During the great epidemics, wars, and horrendous exterminations, there were actual olfactory territories that united everyone in the same fatal breath. It was not until the Twentieth century that death went from being a collective event to a private, solitary one, something that occurred in the hospital.

This marked the transmutation of the odor of death to something clinical, disinfected, frozen in its processes of decomposition. It placed a distance that was also olfactory between us and this mortal event, as wrote Michel Foucault.

That death had something to do with the exhalation of the air in the body was believed since the times of the ancient Egyptians. The nose and mouth of the deceased or the onlookers have always been plugged or covered. In periods of large epidemics and contagions, those who went to visit the sick or dying wore a sort of beak filled with essences, a manifestation of the belief that the breath of the dying could bring death to them as well. Odor was thus believed to be a cause rather than an effect of death. It was a volatile and invisible death, all the more terrible because of its ubiquity and the unavoidable necessity of inhaling.

Separate the Dwelling Place of the Dead from Those of the Living

The separation of the odor of the dead from that of the living is a cardinal element in burial rites: embalming, entombment, cremation. They all entail the same methods and techniques as those used for processing the ingredients and extracting essences for perfumes: exsiccation, *enfleurage*, distillation. The Egyptian embalmment rituals, carried out to achieve synchrony with the eternal present, emptied the body of its earthly humors and stuffed it with fragrances, divine balsams such as myrrh, and resins such as storax.

In the "house of purification" the embalmment process was performed beginning with the extraction of the brain through the nose followed by removal of the viscera. The body was not completely emptied; the heart and the kidneys remained inside. The body once thus emptied was pickled by the embalmer (*taricheute*) in a sort of brine (*patron*), macerating for some thirty-five days. The body was tinted with henna, red for the men and yellow for women, and then filled with tampons soaked in resins and unguents. Storax was applied to the entire surface of the body and then poured into the cranium through the nostrils. Linen or other cloth wrappings were also soaked in storax, coated with spices and wrapped around the body. The mummy was then placed in a sarcophagus, the "house of the deceased", which, as such, adhered to the architectural styles of the various epochs, with a lid that was analogous to a "palace façade".

The Egyptians were incredible architects and refined perfumers, and perhaps this is why we are led to interpret the sarcophaguses, and also the pyramids, as huge perfume packages *ante litteram*.

The Nose of Architecture

The pyramid is the standard form used to imagine the structure of a perfume and its correspondence to the human body is evident as it was in Ancient Egypt. The olfactory pyramid is divided into three parts: top, middle or heart, and bottom or base. When you smell a perfume, the top notes, at the tip of

SEPULTURE RACINE

the pyramid, are the first you notice. Since they are the most volatile, they are also the first to disappear (citrusy, fruity, spiced). The middle notes (floral) are the next ones to emerge, followed by the bottom notes (woody, musky, amber), which are the most persistent.

The Temple of Luxor is considered to be a key for understanding the origin of the western tradition of alchemy. The hereafter was the "eternal present", not just an instant that connected the past to the future but a permanent condition without projection. Writing on the studies of R. A. Schwaller, who dedicated twelve years of his life to the hieroglyphics in the Luxor Temple, George H. Dodd and Steve Van Toller said that in the eternal present time does not flow, it is eternally stopped in the instant that the divinities and the spirits performed the mythical gesture of entering directly in contact with human beings.

The Egyptians had knowledge of the anatomical form of the cranium. The nose was called *fnde*, and the cranium *shtyy nt fnd*, or "hall of the nose", "sanctuary of the nose". According to Dodd and Van Toller, the fact that the Egyptians believed that the nose was a sort of sanctuary gives us insights into the corresponding sanctuary in the Temple of Luxor. Schwaller studied the anatomical structure of the nose and saw that if we placed the longitudinal section of the cranium over the plan of the temple, the olfactory senses corresponded to Room V, while the olfactory bulb and the frontal cerebral lobes corresponded to Room XII. The wall separating these two rooms corresponded to the cribiform plate of the ethmoid bone, through which the olfactory nerves reach the olfactory bulb.

Schwaller concluded that Room V, the sanctuary of the sense of smell, was where the sacred ceremony of the anointment of the pharaoh with scented oils was performed. He also noted that on the east wall of this room, corresponding anatomically to the area of the forehead where the olfactory bulb is lodged, the list of the oils and

Père Lachaise Cemetery, Paris (photo by A. Perliss, 2005)

scents to be applied to the pharaoh's forehead was engraved twice. The pharaoh's crown is depicted precisely in correspondence to the zone of the cranium, and it is surmounted by a rearing cobra, symbol of the sense of smell and capacity for judgment. If Schwaller's theory is correct, the Temple of Luxor would be an architectural representation of the olfactory system.

The Architecture of the Nose

The nose is central. It protrudes into space from the center of the face and connects all other facial orifices. The nose's forward protrusion is counterbalanced by the skull's backward protrusion at the occipital lobe. In the average or idealized face, the vertical position of the tip of the nose and the width of the nostrils are in Golden Section proportion to the brow line, mouth-line and the vertical and horizontal dimensions of the entire face, from chin to hairline and across the cheekbones. The nasal chamber's vaulted ceiling is supported by the ever-growing septum, a vertical wall that divides the chamber down the middle. The septum is the nose's central axis, arcing with an almost imperceptible transition from its bone foundation to a cartilage cap. Internally this bell-shaped cap has two rising symmetrical spirals, resembling the hydrodynamic, vorticoid form of liquid jets.

The ethmoid bone, the nose's bridge, is a crux of the face. For Alberto Giacometti, who spent decades painting and sculpting heads dead-on, the junction of the nose's bridge and the brow was the key to the face; he felt that if he could capture that bit of anatomy that the rest of the head would fall into place. The nostrils, the nose's entryway, are, like the eyes and ears, in a symmetrical pair for depth perception. Studies with brain imaging have shown nostril-specific localization of odors. Although they work in stereo for spatial perception, there is always one nostril that is more active. In two hour cycles the activity passes from one side to the other. The nostril's hair lined surface acts as a screen, filtering out dust or insects.

Ascending up the nasal cavity in three tiered

pairs are the turbinates. Spirals repeat themselves in the nose's shape in general, and specifically in the triplicate turbinates' shell-like forms, or *conchas*. The spiral twits the air currents into vortexes, rolling them into a maximum amount of contact with the cleansing mucus membrane that lines all internal nasal surfaces. By the same token, airborne olfactory elements also rifle along the interior, optimizing their contact with sensory receptors. Mucus, a watery, protein and carbohydrate slick, captures dust and evacuates it with a constant ciliary's flow backward towards the pharynx. The wetness of mucus also facilitates transmission of electrochemical olfactory *stimuli*. Whereas a turbine generates energy, the turbinates generate mucus. They oscillate between shrinking and swelling, dryness and wetness to acclimatize the air and purify it before it further enters the body. This regulation is maintained by the autonomic system, responsible for other autopilot bodily systems such as digestion, blood pressure and heart rate.

The sinuses are four pairs of chambers flanking the nose. The cleansing, saline liquid mucus runs through them, circulated by cilia, tiny fluttering hair-like structures. About a pint of this fluid passes through the sinuses daily in the body's effort to decontaminate its incoming air. The contaminated mucus runs down the back of the pharynx and into the stomach where it is purified. Once the incoming air has been cleaned and acclimatized, it rushes downward into the many branches of the upside-down-tree-shape of the lungs.

The nasal cavity and the oral cavity are like a duplex, separated by the hard-palate roof of the mouth. Because of this proximity, certain features normally considered in the mouth's domain, such as taste and speech, actually derive from this duplex configuration: a major part of flavor perception is an olfactory message; and the voice's sound is shaped by the resonance in the nasal cavity's vaulted ceiling.

The nose is really an antechamber, a loading dock for air and odor. Air is sucked down and olfactory signals shoot up. Olfactory nerves send electrochemical messages to the olfactory bulb in the primitive part of the brain. The messages that enter the brain are wired to a series of systems. The limbic system, our emotional center, memory, and direction are all directly influenced by olfactory information.

According to Eastern notions of bodily mechanics, the energy that charges the air, *chi* in China or *prana* in India, is received by the olfactory bulb. Both cultures have developed refined breathing techniques with the intent of harnessing this circulating energy. Yogic breathing involves the intake of air in one nostril and exhaling through the other so as to effect different parts of the nervous system. Inhaling relays external olfactory information to the brain, but exhaling relays internal olfactory information, as molecules from the lungs pass nasal scent receptors while exiting. This internal information allows the body to create a biofeedback loop, regulating itself according to messages from the lungs as well.

Alchemy and Pharmacy

Precisely because it abuts the territory of death, the realm of odors has mainly been frequented by magic and religion, by alchemists and monks, who developed medicines and drugs during the Middle Age to treat both body and soul with the same potions. Those outside of these two ambits who manifested some interest in the world of odors was looked upon with suspicion and even, in the Dark Ages, condemned to burn at the stake as happened with witches.

It is no accident that one of the world's most celebrated producers of scents in 1221 was the Officina Farmaceutica di Santa Maria Novella, established in Florence by Dominican friars who cultivated medicinal herbs to treat the sick and dying. The history of this institution is emblematic of the Western world's approach to odors. Initially private and monastic, around the Seventeenth century it was opened to the public and in subsequent centuries expanded its trade all the way to China, Russia and India, uniting redemptive and commercial interests along the same route. The Officina later changed from a religious to a laic institution, although it still possesses today that mystical and solemn aura typical of monasteries.

The basic apparatus of alchemists and doctors was one and the same, the alembic. The uncertain genealogy of the word – *al-Ambik* has a dual etymology, Greek and Arab – made its entry into the West for the first distillations less "suspect". It was composed of a recipient into which the ingredient was placed and heated. The vapors were then condensed under a domed cap with the resulting liquid, known as "essence", was collected in another receptacle.

Today the process is much less "alchemical" because there are methods, such as headspace analysis, that can measure odors in a place without necessarily needing to extract them using the traditional processes. It uses an apparatus with a sort of bell jar covering the object or the area to be analyzed. A process of vacuum extraction draws molecules into the air of the "headspace", which is then analyzed to determine the identity of the odor. This method cannot be applied in all cases, while a universally applicable method is one of the ambitions of anyone who manifests an interest in the world of odors.

Grenouille, the protagonist in the celebrated work *Perfume* by Patrick Süskind,

"tried for instance to distill the odor of glass, the clayey, cool odor of smooth glass, something a normal human being cannot perceive at all. He got himself both window glass and bottle glass and tried working with it in large pieces in fragments, in slivers, as dust – all without the least success. He distilled brass, porcelain, and leather, grain and gravel. He distilled plain dirt. Blood and wood and fresh fish. His own hair. By the end he was distilling water from the Seine, the distinctive odor of which seemed to him worth preserving. He believed that with the help of the alembic he could rob these materials of their characteristic odors, just as could be done with thyme, lavender and caraway seeds."

Putrescine and Cadaverine

The odor of death is certainly the most tangible perception of entropy, of that inexorable and irreversible loss of energy released by a decomposing body in the form of a gas.

Humors by Sara Manazza

Blood, phlegm, black bile, and yellow bile are the four humors that make up the human body according to the theory of humors. The four humors described by Hypocrites in the Third century BC and adopted by Galen in the Second century AD are liquids that circulate in the body, a mix of fluids with sensory characteristics close to those of the four natural elements. They are humid or dry, hot or cold, they have a temperature, a color, and a character. The balance of the four humors determines the individual's state of physical or mental health. If the mix of humors goes awry, like an egg in mayonnaise, the vapors and exhalations that cause the dyscrasia have to be vented from the organism. Superfluities have to be sweated out, evacuated, bled, or cauterized. It was as if for centuries people had "soggy bodies".

Variations in the humors, or the dominance of one over the others not only determines the state of health of the body, but also gives rise to four well-defined "psychological" characteristics or temperaments, the limiting constitutions of the individual's character: if blood prevails, a jovial, hot, and humid humor, the temperament is sanguine; if phlegm prevails, a sluggish, humid, and cold humor, the person is phlegmatic; if black bile dominates, a melancholic, cold, and dry element, the person is melancholic; and if yellow bile is abundant, an irascible, dry, and hot humor, the person is irascible.

The relation between humor and temperament is not as banal and straightforward as it might seem because the factors that determine it have many nuances and are not entirely predictable or clear. In fact, the four constitutions, as in the case of the individual's physical and mental equilibrium, are affected by various bio-geographical factors. These include the time of day, the change of seasons, the climate, diet, age, the geographic area, etc. For example, the first three hours of the morning and the last hours of the evening are dominated by blood that tends to be in excess in springtime. Yellow bile predominates in the six hours in the middle of the day and in the summer. Black bile surges in the first three hours of the evening, in the last three hours of the afternoon, and in winter. And the six and a half hours of night are dominated by the autumnal humor phlegm. Likewise, each age has its own humor and corresponding temperament: infancy is phlegmatic, youth is sanguine, maturity is wrathful, and old age is melancholic. But these are only to be taken as general indications of limiting cases, that rarely are found in pure form in reality.

What is true is that the extreme simplicity of the theory of the four humors has made it a fundamental theoretical reference point in medicine from ancient times through much of the Seventeenth century. The associated theory of temperaments deeply impregnated 'psychological' conceptions at least up to the Eighteenth century, and continues to endure in some form even today. These two theories are ancient constructs with notable charm and power. In the case of the individual, for example, the doctrine of humors and corresponding temperaments provides not only a framework for assessing one's physical condition, but also furnishes a basis for judging or diagnosing one's psychic or spiritual qualities. This is all the more noteworthy if we think of the artists and writers who consulted physiatrists, surgeons, alchemists, or physiognomists to invent the personality, physical features, and constitution of their characters.

The close connection that has existed and that perhaps continues to exist between bodily and temperamental humors, between medicine and psycho-physiology, is one of the forms of magic that has endured longest over the centuries and offered the strongest resistance to advances in science and medicine. In spite of the fact that the elements dealt with in scientific circles of the Twenty-first century go well beyond the limited number of "four", the allure of a possible or real connection between the body's organic constituents – its viscera and its internal humors, which physically saturate it – and the psychological predisposition and growth of the individual still exerts a seductive power. This is perhaps because the ancient idea still rings true, the one that states that "the blood that surrounds the heart is thought". If taken in both the physical and psychic sense, in the organic and emotional sense, they are not so far apart from one another after all.

estate
fuoco
bile gialla

caldo   freddo

primavera
aria
sangue

autunno
terra
bile nera

umido   secco

inverno
acqua
flegma

**Schema grafico
della teoria umorale**

However, in the interplay between the rhythms of life and those of death, perhaps the most interesting information is given to us by the molecules of putrescine ($C_4H_{12}N_2$) and cadaverine ($C_5H_{14}N_2$). These molecules are responsible for the smell of rotting flesh that accompanies the decomposition of organic material. But what is interesting is that the same molecules are part of the characteristic odor of semen: in olfactory terms, death and conception are closely linked in a continuum.

Perhaps instinctively this vital continuity in the death-putrefaction-rebirth was perceived in rural cultures where the odor of excrement was not cursed, but welcomed, received willingly for its fertilizing mission: the benefits and drawbacks balanced each other out. With the emergence of the industrial city, the various processes of production, transformation, and consumption were inexorably separated. The natural cycle became forced by the driving rhythms of the machines. Inevitably the processes of assimilation became congested and the first waste dumps were created.

The industrial era caused a serious case of indigestion for the cities, imposing the need to manage wastes, to contain stenches, to send away excrement, and to hide excretions from houses, *piazzas*, and streets. The underlying continuity that made the natural odor of death "tolerable" was finally broken to make way for one of the most frequent conceptions of urban utopia: the scented city.

Dosages and Concentrations

The relationship with odors depends on the smeller's judgment (taste, quality, memory) and on the odor's duration (repeated stimuli lead to inurement) and concentration (smells we might recoil from at high concentrations may actually produce a pleasant perfume at low concentrations). This is a well established fact in perfumeries, which may use extracts of excrement, hormonal secretions, or excited animal calculi at low concentrations as indispensable ingredients in their fragrances.

Thus there are no stinks or malodors *per se*; it is all a question of combinations and concentrations. However, any investigation into what might be considered the "stink to end all stinks" reaches the same result: excrement. Within the arms market, the Pentagon has carried out a study to determine what the absolute stink would be. They were looking for something that would trigger the flight response and total disgust in any culture. After years of experimentation with the most horrendous stenches in the world, the unrivalled winner was the US "government standard bathroom malodor". Before it is even recognized by the brain this odor sparks immediate flight in all those subjected to it. It is a combination of odors of various types of excrement which is used mainly to test the effectiveness of deodorants. However the applications are rapidly expanding out of environmental hygiene into the realm of "social hygiene" as possible crowd dispersers to replace tear gas as a means of controlling demonstrations.

Scatology

Roland Barthes stated that written shit does not stink, suggesting that outside of the semantic experience, the smell of feces is among the most nauseating of olfactory experiences.

When the early hominids gave up their quadruped gait to assume a vertical stance, it marked a revolutionary turning point in the perception of geometrical space, but also of olfactory space. The nose was now farther away from the ground, where the highest concentration of odors is found. This distance also led to the loss of familiarity and a change in taste regarding certain odors that were previously considered pleasant but had now become repugnant. On the scale of the individual, this thought is echoed in the theories of Sigmund Freud, who attributed most neuroses and psychoses to the emergence of a disgust for feces. He saw it as an unnatural conditioning that leads children to consider their excrement to be something extraneous to themselves and thus disgusting.

We may draw a parallel between the individual and the city by observing that at a certain point in the growth of a body (whether human or urban) there is always a moment of rising up from the ground, of going from a horizontal to a vertical position, of gaining distance from one's excrement and from the ground surface. The first industrial city produced the skyscraper, a new way of rising from the ground and gaining space above. This was not only a response to high population density, but also a means of escaping from the miasmas of the street, the stenches at ground level. It is no coincidence that Rome, the ancient city *par excellence*, has bequeathed to posterity a symbol of its power in the form of the hydraulic engineering work of the Cloaca Maxima.

We may posit an "excremental age" in architecture when the structures were close and promiscuous with the odors of the ground, of bodies, beasts, and sex, and of feces, which were considered to be a resource in pharmacy and cosmetics. The advent of the industrial age marked the end of this world. It banished the odors of bodies and beasts from the city and its architecture. It elevated whiteness and cleanliness beyond hygienic import to the status of moral values. It ventilated its spaces and exposed them to the light of day as had never happened before.

The work of the early hygienists moved in the direction of isolating excrement. The latrine-towers that seemed inspired as much by chimneys as by D'Arcet's dovecote were public toilets comprising a seat suspended almost in thin air accessed via a metal walkway. Significant progress in construction materials and finishes was made with the advent of smooth surfaces, enamel and lacquer to ensure that air and water would run off unhindered.

In the Orient however another direction was taken. Early on in his short work *In Praise of Shadows*, Jun'ichiro Tanizaki spends a long moment praising the Japanese toilet: "The parlor may have its charms, but the Japanese toilet is a place of spiritual repose. It always stands apart from the main building, at the end of a corridor, in a grove fragrant with leaves and moss. No words can describe that sensation as one sits in the dim light, basking in the faint glow reflected from the shoji, lost in mediation or gazing out at the garden… Here, I suspect, is where haiku poets over the ages have come by a great many of their ideas.

Indeed one could with some justice claim that of all the elements of Japanese architecture, the toilet is the most aesthetic. (Our forebears, making poetry of everything in their lives, transformed what by rights should be the most unsanitary room in the house into a place of unsurpassed elegance, replete with fond associations with the beauties of nature. Compared to Westerners, who regard the toilet as utterly unclean and avoid even the mention of it in polite conversation, we are far more sensible and certainly in better taste.)"

Futurism and Necrophilia

In questions of cleanliness, hygiene, air, and light, the Futurists were true militant fundamentalists. The exaltation of upward and diurnal values against the symbols of night was not merely a manifestation of progress and energy, but also a maniacal way of exorcising death.

According to Eric Fromm, not only a passion for foul smells but also excessive hygiene is one of the character traits of necrophilia. In this sense, Tommaso Filippo Marinetti, in one of the *Manifesti* published in 1910 that laid out the groundwork for Futurism, more than proclaiming innovation seems to be attacking the humors and odors of the body and of architecture: "We aspire to the creation of a non-human type from whom will be extirpated moral pain, goodness, affection, and love, [as they are] no more than poisons eating away at our inexhaustible vital energy, no more than on/off switches to our powerful physiological electricity. While on the other hand in order to overcome biological man we enlist scientific knowledge, especially regarding mechanics, that will give rise to the creation of a new being, the 'non-human type'. This non-human, mechanical type, built for omnipresent speed, will naturally be cruel, omniscient, and combative. The realm of life has become the realm of 'non-life'; people have become 'non-people'. [It is] a world of death. Death is no longer represented by stinking feces and corpses. Now its symbols are clean, gleaming machines; men are no longer attracted to fetid latrines, but to structures in glass and aluminum."

The biology of matter had become an obsession to exorcise with exercises in creativity and design in all fields, especially those where there still was a trace of uncontrolled naturalness. This is clearly exemplified in *Futurist Flora and Plastic Equivalents of Artificial Odors* by Fedele Azari, dedicated to the death of odors and natural flowers which were to be replaced by others designed and created in the laboratory.

But the first signs of this fear of death and excrement together are found in the literature of the late Nineteenth century in a crowning work of literature on the sense of smell, *Au Rebours* by Joris Karl Huysmans, which strongly challenged the olfactory dogma by which natural odors were better than artificial ones. The protagonist, *Des Esseintes*, collects flowers that appear artificial, rejecting those that appear natural and goes to live *au rebours* (counter currently) in a countryside pervaded with the odors of industry, signs of a modernity that favored the artificial as an emblem of progress, perfection, control, and reproducibility.

In support of Fromm's thesis, the architect Bernard Tschumi stated in an interview that the completely white structures of the 1930s represented, on the one hand, society's fears of death and decomposition, and on the other, admiration for the white and desiccated ruins of antiquity. Tschumi hoped that the hypocritical distinction between mind and experience of space in architecture could be overcome, saying that emancipation from taboos such as decomposition and eroticism were among the most interesting ways for transcending this paradigm.

Blood

The odor of violent death is the smell of blood. This is the olfactory experience that most strongly sparks and excites, terrifies, and reawakens the animal that is in all of us. The smell of blood is the smell of aggression, of the violent proximity of death, of primal hand to hand combat.

In the book *The Conquest of Mexico*, Cortés described the unbreathable odor of the Aztec cities. Upon arriving in Tenochtitlan – one of the main cities, with spacious *plazas*, temples, buildings, and luxurious gardens – the sanguinary Spanish soldiers immediately noticed that the air was saturated with human blood. At night, the priests performed bloody rites with animals and people. To accommodate these ceremonies the Aztec cities developed the standard city center that we are all familiar with: broad *plazas* for public gatherings, religious dances, and games. These spaces were built to accommodate all those who remained outside of the pyramid-temples where the sacrificial rites were celebrated. A broad staircase led to the top, from where the priests would hurl down the lacerated bodies of the victims, killed four at a time in precise rituals, from dawn to dusk, four days a week. Blood was everywhere, not only near the sites of the sacrifices, but it was also used to make mortar for buildings and monuments. Cortés wrote that the statues of the Aztec gods were much larger than even a big man. They were made using the seeds and beans that the Aztecs ate. Here they were ground up and mixed with human blood from hearts ripped from the chests of still living victims. The blood was collected and mixed with the seeds and beans until there was enough to build a huge statue. And after the statue had been built they made offerings to it of other hearts from other human victims.

There are numerous places associated with the bloody odor of death: battlefields, sacrificial altars, arenas, and slaughterhouses. If we try to use our imagination to reawaken the odor of blood in which the Roman Coliseum was steeped when the lions tore apart the early Christians, we might have an inkling of the overpowering sensation of excitement, participation, ritual, and madness that pervaded the place. It is the same sensation we may feel today in a *plaza de toros* when the bull, or perhaps the *torero*, is killed in the *corrida*. And perhaps it is the same sensation we have in other places of collective excitement where sooner or later blood begins to flow.

The blood of death and pain has disappeared from our lives. We have frozen that hot, odorous, sticky, and thick blood in our freezers, free of odors or feelings of guilt. We have

absorbed it into deodorized tampons without humors or corporality. We do keep a visual record of blood. We embrace it in films à la Quentin Tarantino, in the emphasis placed on it in others like *Saving Private Ryan* by Steven Spielberg where the sequence of the disembarkation is a gruesome explosion of bodies, blood, and human pulp mixed with the fine sand of Normandy and driven into the nostrils of the audience as a total memento.

For this reason body art shakes us when it embraces blood as a fundamental ingredient in its performances. Any work of Franko B tears at our stomachs and consciences where the flagellated body dripping with blood becomes a canvas, not for beauty or perfection, but for the pain, the love, the hate, the loss, the power, and the fears of the human condition.

Punishment

The electric chair is a theater of cruelty whose odors are perhaps the most extreme statement of this exercise in death. And yet it was introduced in the United States in 1888 because it was considered a more "humane" alternative to hanging. And it is perhaps for this ambition of normalcy that Andy Warhol adopted it as an icon of his times, as a common image to be silk-screened in all its banal violence in *Big Electric Chair* (1967).

It is a strange short-circuit when the inmate is strapped to the chair and moist copper electrodes are fixed to their head and legs. The other end of the wires is connected to an electrical generator that emits 500 to 2000 Volts. The procedure causes visibly devastating effects. The prisoner sometimes convulses forward against the straps. He may urinate, defecate, or vomit blood. The internal organs are burned. The air fills with the smell of burned flesh. It takes no more than ten minutes, but before Lars von Trier's *Dancer in the Dark* (2000), every moment is doused in the tears of the audience watching the jerking body of Selma played by the unmatchable Icelandic artist, Bjork.

Garbage Dump, New York City (photo by G. Hafner, 2000)

Another method, 'inspired' by the use of poison gases in the First World War, was introduced in the United States in the 1920s. Here the prisoner is sealed into a gas chamber. For a period of 8-10 minutes hydrogen cyanide gas is released in the chamber. The gas inhibits the action of respiratory enzymes that transfer oxygen from the blood to the cells. The prisoner usually holds his or her breath at first but is then forced to inhale and dies quickly of asphyxia.

Food

The spaces dedicated to food and its transformation are places of very high entropy, where matter is transformed into something else while dissipating energy and emanating strongly perceptible odors.

The smell of food is also an indicator of its quality and state of conservation, or we might say its relation to the processes of decomposition. In the transformation of food the great actors are bacteria, the vehicles for decomposition. Bacteria are also fundamental ingredients in the alchemy of odors: if they are present in limited numbers they may cause the food to age in particular and delicious ways; if there are too many they decompose the food and render it inedible. Many important food transformation processes such as aging, fermentation, leavening, etc., would not exist without bacteria.

To slow down the decomposition of food, and also to cover up the flavor of food gone bad, spices were imported from the Orient, finding their most perverse applications during the Baroque period. Baroque cuisine, usually based on game, tasted strongly of confectioned corpse, embalmed in honey, flavorings, spices, and balsamic vinegar. Baroque cuisine was not a happy exercise, but an almost macabre ritual of death (the animal) by the living (the person). This theme brings to mind still lifes, especially those by Caravaggio, with pallid and emaciated fruit that looked like it emanated that sickly-sweet smell of fruit going bad.

There are designers and artists who are not averse to odors and the reek of decomposing organic matter. Not only are they not afraid, they actually use the stink as an ingredient in their projects. One example is Gaetano Pesce, who uses perishable works in his exhibitions. Among the best known are the olfactory experiences at the *Made in Italy* exhibition, where he displayed typical foods and drinks that changed over time, offering the visitor an unusual and unforgettable experience in olfaction.

Food flavorings represents one of the most flourishing industries and one that will merit attention in the upcoming decades, as prophesized by Philip Dick in *Ubik*:

"Tired of lazy tastebuds? Has boiled cabbage taken over your world of food? That same old, stale, flat, Monday-morning odor no matter how many dimes you put into your stove? Ubik changes all that; Ubik wakes up food flavor, puts hearty taste back where it belongs, and restores fine food smell. One invisible puff-puff whisk of economically priced Ubik banishes compulsive obsessive fears that the entire world is turning into clotted milk, worn-out tape recorders and obsolete iron-cage elevators, plus other, fur-ther, as-yet- unglimpsed manifestations of decay."

Eau de New Orleans

When Noah opened the window of his Ark to see if it had stopped raining, he must have smelled something that has to be called the olfactory essence of the world, the total fragrance. There was all of creation in the water on which the Ark was floating: people, animals, plants, everything that had been submerged. Who knows how long it took for all that water to dry up, for the mud to become solid ground, and for that primordial odor to be removed from the nostrils of the survivors. The experience of death through the odor of stagnant water is strong, as if that hypo-oxygenated solution teeming with bacteria were the airborne expression of the end. Again in Süskind's book *Perfume*, Paris is a city with mortal humors:

"The thousands of odors and stenches oozed out as if from thousands of festering boils. Not a breeze stirred. The vegetables in the market stalls shriveled up. Meat and fish rotted. Tainted air hung in the narrow streets. Even the river seemed to have stopped flowing, to have stagnated. It stank."

The idea of water that submerges brings to mind the *tsunami* that hit the coasts of Thailand and Indonesia in 2003, that shifted Sumatra, that drowned thousands of people and other lives, that flooded houses and buildings, that submerged a vast part of Southeast Asia. It brings to mind Hurricane Katerina that hit New Orleans in 2005, killing people, destroying buildings and roads. It makes us perceive with our noses the endless cycle of the ecosystem.

A project by 2A+P titled *Swamp Project for the Ecocenter at the Nakdong River* was developed with the intention of creating a structure that rests on and sinks into shifting sands. The building lacks a foundation and floats like a bowl immersed in the ground. The center, dug to the same level as the river, is in direct continuity with the natural soil. A thick canebrake of artificial reeds consolidates the structure and supports the roof, while its openings allow air to circulate, allowing the system to breathe in a natural process of ventilation supplemented with fans.

The sand dune mutates into an inhabitable swamp, an underground space that encloses a microclimate. It is an inhabitable greenhouse in close relation with the natural environment into which the visitor is immersed down to the water table. It is a sublevel experience in the exhibition space, an exploration of the deep soil. *Swamp* is an invisible work of architecture lacking any formal value. It is an organic system, an operating laboratory to study the ecological and environmental conditions of the Nakdong River area.

Volatile Organic Compounds

The olfactory pollution of contemporary cities is due to three fundamental causes: difficulty in disposing of wastes, air pollution from car exhaust, and a lack both of adequate public policies regarding odors and the management of air scenting operations.

The air we breath contains Volatile Organic Compounds (VOC) which are literally lethal. We perceive them as a pungent sensation as they excite the trigeminal nerve, which has the fundamental olfactory role of alerting us to danger. VOCs are carbon-containing molecules that we perceive only at relatively high concentrations. However, they are gradually released by most of the materials used in architecture and design. These include construction materials, furnishing elements (fabricated wooden panels, particle board, paper, synthetic textiles, carpets, plastic coatings, insulation, polyurethane foams, glues, lacquers, resins, moth repellents/killers, wood preservatives, etc.), and detergents for cleaning interiors. They are also released during combustion processes associated with kerosene heaters, gas stoves, or smoking.

Other factors that affect air quality are the electrostatic properties of certain products such as carpets and some synthetic wallpapers, and the hygroscopic characteristics of certain materials that absorb odors like sponges. Certain underground works by Emilio Ambasz turned out to contain high concentrations of radon gas released from the surrounding soils, a serious drawback which required control measures in subsequent works.

However, a careful analysis of the volatility of dusts may contribute to the olfactory and visual qualities of certain spaces. In Annette Gigon and Mike Guyer's early works for the restoration and expansion of the Oskar Reinhart Collection they mixed limestone from the Jura and copper into the concrete. This creates a surface that rapidly becomes red and then green. The materials used to build the Switching Box at the Zurich train station contain iron oxide pigments that have the same chemical basis and also the same odor as the dust left on the rails by the trains.

Dust

Dust carries the odor of passing time and of the material that produced it. In his book *La polvere nell'arte* [Dust in Art], the art critic Elio Grazioli traces the historic presence in art of formless matter, of the entropic materialization of the passage of time. In its initial stages he sees it as a negative manifestation, but then starting with Marcel Duchamp and his *Dust Breeding*, he sees it as an expressive and positive ingredient in art. Since then, writes Grazioli, "dust is a trace", and thus an inscription and a narrative.

Another paramount book in grasping the relation between dust and our times is Marco Belpoliti's *Crolli* [Collapses], which examines the period bracketed by the collapses of two pieces of architecture – the Berlin Wall and the World Trade Center – in end-of-the-millennium art. Belpoliti writes about the incredible coincidence that led to Wolfgang Staehle's work *Untitled* in 2001. The artist was in New York with an installation that involved setting up a number of video cameras in various parts of the world. One of them was focused on the Twin Towers on the morning of September 11, 2001. It was unintentional live coverage. He caught everything. And so the dust that rose thickly over Manhattan and invaded its streets, buildings, and apartments, the dust that fell upon those fleeing the scene of disaster, the dust that blanketed cars, benches, parks, and trees, that thick, gray dust, the volatilized cement,

asbestos, paper, and objects that had been in the towers, became part of the work of art. The dust produced by the collapse of the Towers contained the Towers themselves. It is the trace and the index of their collapse. The air and the wind carried it far away until it was dispersed in the Earth's atmosphere. Now it is everywhere.

Art Spiegelman drew the towers in his *In the Shadow of No Towers*, telling the story of September 11th with the Towers pulverizing in the incandescent tones of fire. He was reminded of his father trying to describe the odor of the smoke at Auschwitz. The best his father could come up with was "indescribable". And that is also the best way to define the air in lower Manhattan after September 11th. It was full of asbestos, biphenyls, lead, dioxin, and bits of people. It was a witch's brew that made Chernobyl seem like a spa.

In the nostrils of those who were in Manhattan that morning there remains the memory of an unbreathable odor that still persists undiluted. It is the odor of the dust that had once been the Towers, built between

1966 and 1972 based on plans by the Japanese-American architect Minoru Yamasaki, mixed together with all the lives that were lost in the collapse.

Odorless Death

The most terrible and treacherous smell of death is non-odor.

Killing by means of gas has been used many times in history. According to the writings of Polybius around 187 BC, the Romans used poisonous fumes to flush the defenders of Corinth from their underground tunnels. Asphyxiating gases were used during First World War composed of hydrocyanic acid, chloropicrin, arsine, and other components.

But it was the murder of Jews in the gas chambers of the concentration camps during Second World War that made clear the atrocity of this type of death and proved beyond a shadow of a doubt that the odorless is more lethal. The gas was called Zyklon B, a mixture of hydrocyanic acid and other poisons produced by the Tesch & Stabenow company officially as an insecticide.

It is an odor that risks being forgotten by those who have had no direct experience, but one that belongs to the survivors as writes Erri de Luca in *I colpi dei sensi*: "To that humanity exterminated with Zyklon B gas, whose odor has poisoned our century, and that no one knows."

Unfortunately the list of lethal substances for killing enemies or presumed enemies is as long as it is abominable: napalm, nerve gas, depleted uranium, white phosphorus, Agent Orange, just to name the best known. The manufacturers of these "smart" weapons call them "non-lethal" – Zyklon B was labeled as an herbicide in – because they are supposed to be sprayed on enemies not to kill them but to "incapacitate" them. They are gases with a tranquilizing or an anesthetic effect that include among their official ingredients valium and opium derivatives and who knows what other non-declared ingredients. They represent one of the most powerful markets in the world and not even the International Treaty on Chemical and Bacteriological Weapons can regulate it.

In 2002 the air conditioning system of one of
the most beautiful opera houses in Moscow
was transformed into a vector of death. A
commando unit of Cechen terrorists barri-
caded in the Dubrovka Theater held hundreds
of people hostage without any possibility of
official negotiations. A "non lethal" gas was
released into the air conditioning system that
resulted in the deaths of 120 people. Of the
survivors, or the "incapacitated", we have had
no further news.

Perception
by Erminia
De Luca, 2005

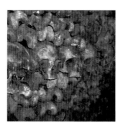

THE CATACOMBS, PARIS – Twenty meters below the street level of Paris, 14th arrondissement, a serpentine tunnel meanders along a distance of almost eight hundreds meters. At the tunnel entrance is the warning: "Stop, this is the empire of the dead", beyond which lie the dried bones of approximately six million permanent residents. The first bone piles came from the Cemetery of the Innocents, in the center of Paris, which, after almost one thousand years of use, was evacuated for sanitary purposes. The catacombs piqued curiosity from the beginning and hosted such illustrious guests as Francis I, emperor of Austria, and Napoleon III with his son.

PHILIPPE RAHM – He is a Paris based architect. He was one half of the former design team Décosterd & Rahm, which disbanded in 2004. His works have presented at the Venice Biennale, the Foundation Cartier, and the Centre Georges Pompidou in Paris, among others. He was a fellow at the *Villa Medici, Académie de France* in Rome in 2000. He is Master of the Diploma Unit at the AA School in London.

MAURICE ROUCEL – He is one of the fragrance industry's most successful perfumers, responsible for such works as Hermès' *24*, Faubourg's *Tocade*, Gucci's *Envy*, DKNY's *Be Delicious*, *L'Instant de Guerlain*, and *Musc Ravageur* for Frederic Malle.

MR – Naturally during decomposition, the body releases a lot of chemicals, which are generally ammonia derivatives. Some are very, very strong and disgusting.

PR – A book by Friedrich Nietzsche explores what is beauty and what is not beauty. This book is more a question of the odor of death. He says that if we define something as awful, it is because there is the smell of death. Its chemical relationship reminds us that it is dangerous to the body, that it could corrupt the body. it is the idea that decomposition is not beauty. It is not an aesthetical but a chemical relationship with the smell of death.

MR - Yeah, the smell of decomposition is dangerous. It's like when you smell gas – the gas itself is odorless; we have to put a scent product inside, so that when you smell the scent you know that there is a leak. You can perfume everything. In Istanbul a Muslim king built a mosque and put real animal musk inside the cement. It still smells one thousand two hundred years later. A piece of wood or paper or clothes can be injected with micro encapsulation so that every time you move you break the microscopic capsules that release perfume. Technologically you can perfume wallpaper and this smell could last for years and years. The problem with scented wallpaper is that it is impossible to change the smell - you have to loose the wallpaper and that's a bore.

PR – A key question in looking at the relationship between perfume and architecture is to understand whether perfume could be an architectural element that could evolve or change, like the air...

MR – You have to fix time with perfume. Imagine perfume as an orchestra and all the raw materials inside of the bottle are all playing at the same time. Little by little, as time goes on, the lightest molecules will disappear, and the strong molecules, very heavy ones such as vanilla, sandalwood, will stay. According to the evaporation you have to seek the accord; and it has to be nice. You cannot build a perfume without a foundation. Perfume is like a symphony. You put together different molecules and there you have an accord. You have to be playing this accord for one and a half hours; this means that you have to make it beautiful, long lasting.

PR – I did a project that explored the question of spirituality and odor. It was also a kind of provocation about the disappearance of space, of the symbolic aspects of architecture inside a spiritual place. Before the church was built like the cross and the cross was the body of Christ. So you go inside the body of Christ when you go in the church, you eat the *ostia* and you eat the body of Christ. You are doing a body exchange with Christ. When Modernism arrives at the beginning of the 20th century, this symbolic aspect disappears because in Modernism we don't want this symbolic aspect of architecture anymore, we just want that form follows function. So the first church at the beginning of the century was like a factory and there were some polemics. Maybe it was difficult for people not to have symbolic meaning in church architecture, so it is the light in architecture that becomes the symbolic aspect. It's a paradox that symbolism, excluded from modern architectural form, has found refuge in the treatment of light. If you look at the Le Corbusier church there is a very precise way to put the light inside the space. Another example is the church designed by Tadao Ando: the form of the church is like a modern factory, yet the symbolic representation of the cross returns, no longer in the form of the church, but in the form of the light. There is no more formal design for the church, but it becomes a symbolic light. Following this process whereby shape and form disappear, we also tried to erase the question of light and just follow the question of air. We created the *Buon Odore del Cristo*, with the perfumers Christopher Sheldrake and Christine Nagel from *Quest International*, because there is *l'odore de sainte* when he was dead. They opened the tomb and you could feel a good odor. In the Bible or in different texts are descriptions of the odor of Christ.

MR – You are talking about the Gospels… The body of Christ was a little bit out of odor, because it was written at least forty years after his death. At the same time, we are talking about religion and religion is a political power. When you build a big church you feel small inside the cathedral. The smell of incense makes you feel more humble; the light, a special kind of lighting, makes you feel even more humble; the music too, when you listen, especially to the big organ at Notre Dame, you feel even more humble. That's to put

you in a special state of mind where you can be manipulated. I don't want to discuss politics here, but they are playing on the different senses to put you in a position of inferiority.

PR – With Modernism there was a problem because the religious space was not symbolic, and so it begins not to humble you. It becomes like a factory, you go inside and there is this place… In the end we wanted to stop this and just to produce the perfume. It was the same as the cross of the body of Christ, but you go inside this odor. It was like a disappearing inside Modernism, of the symbolic aspect - you go inside of the body and you smell the odor of Christ. The formal aspect of the church becomes something that you breathe, but you are not going inside, you are drawn inside.

MR – There is a question of one's upbringing when you smell something. If you give, let's say, to an Eskimo, the smell of incense, he has no reaction. You react to it because you have been trained by that since you are a young guy. Like with soap, you are educated that its smell means clean, it's a question of upbringing.

PR – Here it was different. In this it was more of an idea to show the limit of Modernism.

MR – The perfume *Pleasures* by Estée Lauder is a perfume that works in New York but not in Paris. I don't have a rational explanation; maybe it is because of the different cultural taste. You have so many parameters. If I am supposed to work for a Spanish brief I have to take care of Spanish taste. You cannot have an international style because it is impossible to please everybody. First the difference was more geographical, now it is more social. Increasingly there is a social stratification where there could be more difference between a guy living in Paris and another in the south of France, than between someone in Paris and someone in Tokyo. Their spirit, their way of living, the products they might use – today they have more in common sociologically. You cannot define it precisely, you define it by experience. Just as you cannot always anticipate the effect of a raw material's structure. You have always surprises, and you are always obliged to experience. The more you experience the more you know.

EMOTIONS
AND RITES

Architecture as Urns

Odors are often bridges between the here and now and the hereafter and it is perhaps for this reason that the religious institutions bought up incense, candles, unguents, and balsams of all types as instruments to guarantee their monopoly of souls. Offered as a gift to the gods by all past civilizations, perfume spiritually elevates and renders divine the body, it transforms sacred places into urns.

The history of religious sites is steeped in a mixture of purifying scents and cadaverous stenches, of heaven and earth, of ecstasy and horror, of ascension and inhumation, of sublimation (the upper reaches, heaven, the balsamic) and decomposition (the lower reaches, the grave, the underground, hell). The olfactory compositions of these sacred sites have never been random. We might consider them to be bona fide invisible architectures superimposed forcefully and intentionally over the formal, luminous, and acoustic ones. Their purpose was to serve as an emotional guide for the faithful in order to psychologically condition them and orient their participation.

In his *Journal of the Plague Year*, published in 1722, Daniel Defoe wrote that "If we came to go into a church when it was anything full of people, there would be such a mixture of smells at the entrance that it was much more strong, though perhaps not so wholesome, than if you were going into an apothecary's or druggist's shop. In a word, the whole church was like a smelling-bottle; in one corner it was all perfumes, in another, aromas, balsams, and variety of drugs and herbs; in another, salts and spirits, as every one was furnished for their own preservation."

In architectural terms, the movement that most strongly marked the shift from the urn to the ampoule was the *Glassarckitecktur* of Bruno Taut and Paul Scheerbart. As opposed to the architecture that preceded it, which favored an urn-like structure, i.e., a dark, enclosed container with no ventilation, the "glass architecture" introduced the idea of the transparent, openable, and breathable ampoule. These were the same

Shiva Altar, Narlai, Rajasthan (photo by A. Perliss, 2003)

53

years (1914-1920) that glass became an indispensable material for packaging industrially produced perfume and extending its use throughout society.

Taut's Glass Pavilion at the Cologne Werkbund Exposition in 1914 was made in a similar manner to the perfume bottles created some years earlier by René Lalique for the perfumer Françoise Coty. These were the years when Adolf Loos renovated the façade of the Knize perfumery, whose packaging was designed by Ernst Dryden, a student of Gustav Klimt.

Odor of Sanctity

If fragrance is a vehicle for the divine, then God is a dispenser of essences (and existences), the sacred is scented, and its places are impregnated with odors. Leaving one's body and being transported into the hereafter by a perfume is a positive sign for any culture or religion, whether it be by incense, candles, wreaths of flowers, or the sandalwood branches used for traditional cremations.

The Ancient Egyptians believed that those who breathed the breath of Osiris would emanate a delicate perfume. Those who visited him after their death would rest in peace because they had breathed his myrrh and incense scented breath. The association between odor and sanctity was so explicit that the priests of the cult of Osiris chewed cedar gum to perfume their breath and create a scented aura of sacredness, the same concept we find in toothpastes and oral hygiene products.

The Greeks practiced a funerary toilet that involved washing the body of the deceased with scented oils and wrapping it in scented sheets before sending it off on its journey to the Elysian Fields. In the pre-Christian world the invisible presence of the divine was sensed in the indescribable smell of ambrosia. In Christianity as well, sanctity emanated a scent. Christ arose from the dead amidst the scent of myrrh and aloe, with which he had been anointed after the Deposition. And hence the wounds and stigmata of the saints did not smell of rotting flesh, but emanated a delicate perfume like those of Saint Francis or Saint Clare, or smelled of violets like those of Padre Pio.

In Christianity, a scented body, even if poor or

ragged, was a positive sign and marked perhaps even a vocation for saintliness. Thus the deceased prior to burial are also perfumed so that they emanate sanctity, cheating in some way the natural processes of putrefaction. But the Christian church has vacillated in the use of perfumes as a bridge to the divine. While the church condemned the personal, Dionysian use of perfume and limited the use of scents in its own rites to incense and flowers, it also promoted more urbane religious rituals and celebrations that were bona fide olfactory performances. In the rite of *Corpus Domini* the streets are paved in a multicolored scented carpet of flower petals for the passage of the "Body of Christ".

There is a work by J. G. Décosterd and P. Rahm titled *Il Buon odore di Cristo* [The Sweet Odor of Christ] created for the exhibition *Dal Paradiso all'Inferno* [From Heaven to Hell] put on by Giacinto Di Pierantonio at the Fondazione Bevilacqua La Masa in Venice in 2004 that fully expressed this odor of sanctity. It was an upside-down mushroom hanging from the ceiling all the way to the floor that emanated the smell of incense, myrrh, and cinnamon. The idea is that the holy odors, impregnated with sanctity, are veritable placebos: they soothe, beatify, heal…

Earthly Paradise and Heavenly Garden

If the hereafter is a scented realm, then the iconography faithfully adheres to the metaphors: of heaven with fine and crisp freshly scented air, of a garden of earthly appearance but much more luxuriant and sweet, of the Elysian Fields with five hundred scented fountains, or of the great plain.

The earthly paradise described in the book of Genesis is a garden that offers all that could be desired, where all is in flower and bursting with ripe fruit. We all know what happened in the end. The garden of Eden has remained an expression of the desires and the damnation of much of humanity, at least among the Abrahamitic religions, which have continued to recreate it on Earth in all sorts of versions and dimensions. In the Old Testament another garden is described in the *Song of Songs*. It was an enclosed, sealed garden, "[…] an orchard of pomegranates, with the most exquisite fruits; camphire, with spikenard […] and saffron; calamus and cinnamon, with all trees of frankincense; myrrh and aloes, with all the chief spices […]" that evoke the virginity of the beloved. But it was the Hanging Gardens of Babylon that attempted to make this dream a concrete reality.

The idea of the celestial garden is also found in other religions. Paradisiacal hereafter is a garden, then the most appropriate symbol is a tomb rising from a field of flowers. The Alhambra Gardens, conceived as a metaphor for paradise and its foretaste on Earth, are an interpretation from the spiritual yet sensual Islamic civilization, which concentrates sophisticated beauty and light hedonism.

A work by Décosterd and Rahm sought to bring this idea into the olfactory realm. For New Year's 2003 they created an installation at the Fondation Cartier pour l'Art Contemporain in Paris titled *Paradise Now*, based on the contemporary spatiality of the ineffable. With no materiality or physical limits other than odor, *Paradise Now* was an inter-religious version of the earthly paradise or the celestial garden, which coincide quite well in the olfactory dimension: musk, aloe, milk, and honey, and wine as fragrances of the Islamic paradise with an extra touch of incense for the Christian heaven.

Gardens

The garden has always been the place for constructing emotions through rites, planting, care, and harvest. By definition it is a grand bouquet composed of a particular combination of plant, tree, and flower species, varying with the seasons and the arrangement of the scent sources. It constitutes on the natural scale what the perfumers seek to capture in a bottle.

The history of French, English, or Italian gardens is much too broad to address thoroughly in this book, but each of us can use our imaginations to grasp the olfactory orgy that can be breathed in each of these types of garden. The plan for a garden is extremely complex because the invisible dimension and variable dynamics of odors are more evident here than elsewhere. The antithesis of the blooming garden is the

Zen rock garden. Here plants are replaced by stones and the soil by granite or clear marble sand. The Zen garden does not seek to seduce the senses but to invite meditation.

To express how the garden reveals itself still today as a space for olfactory design we have looked at works by Petra Blaisse titled *Outside* and a particular Zen garden designed by Yukio Nakagawa

The works of Blaisse are particularly interesting regarding the development of the concept of the contemporary garden. Here the Dutch artist does not maintain the sharp distinction between natural and artificial but instead creates a threshold where the artificial is naturalized and the natural made artificial. One of her current works is the *Library of Trees* in Milan which will include trees of different species as a living archive of scents and essences.

In 2003 Yukio Nakagawa created an installation titled *Onde onirique* [Oneiric Wave] in the Hermès space in Tokyo that remained in place for three months and had all the characteristics of a Zen garden, but it was scented with clouds of lavender laid out on the ground. Seven hun-

dred kilograms of lavender blossoms created lavender and cobalt-blue waves that were arranged together with red, blue, and white bubbles in a dreamlike world that enveloped visitors in a delicate perfume. In another recent work *Tenku Sange* [Paradise], Nakagawa creates a multicolored, scented rain composed of 200,000 tulip petals. The geometric space remains immobile while the olfactory dimension is dynamic.

Secrets

The *Hortus Conclusus* inspired from Chapter 4 of the *Song of Solomon*, "A garden inclosed *is* my sister, *my* spouse; a spring shut up, a fountain sealed […]" not only expressed the idea of a garden but was also a metaphor for virginity. From the architectural standpoint it is a walled garden containing the flowers that are the symbol of paradise. This type provided inspiration for the cloisters in Medieval convents, which are also where the systematic classification of plants was begun.

Damascus is a city full of gardens, but they are all hidden behind high walls. They are invisible to the eyes but not hidden from the sense of smell which allows us to imagine them in all

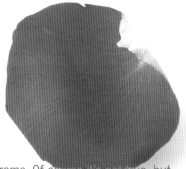

21 Grams by Romina Savi

According to Alejandro Gonzalez Inarritu's film, the soul weighs twenty-one grams. Of course it's not true, but let's pretend it is. And we'll pretend that these recipes for what different people would like those twenty-one grams of soul to contain are also genuine. In their small dosages they contain life, flavor, smells, joy, and sadness.

Antonio, journalist: 9 gr. of acoustic guitar by Pat Metheny, 7 gr. of *Aqua di Bulgari*, 1 gr. of *Atkinson's Lavander*, 3 gr. of Perrier Jouet, 1 gr. of salt, and the residue of bitterness left by life.

Emilio, musician: 4 gr. of Pink Floyd, 4 gr. of Frank Zappa, 4 gr. of Pat Metheny, 4 gr. of Steve Vai, 3 gr. of beer, and 2 gr. of cinnamon to spice the passage into the hereafter.

Filippo, graphic artist: "If perfume is what the soul remembers first of all, then my 21 grams are the intense and overwhelming fragrance of *fragolino* grapes hanging overripe at the end of August from the pergola in the courtyard of my grandparent's house."

Giancarlo, dentist: "My 21 grams are a blend. The basic weave is made of parchment as in my beloved books and menus. Then a bit of Chantilly cream together with the sincere herbaceous notes of a Clos du Mesnil. A fruity mix of oil, basil, tomato, and a very subtle, long finish of Venetian fried liver. Lastly the spiced notes of the musical staff that expresses both Bach and U2…"

Miranda, writer: "21 drops of water and light. One for everything I would like to have done before I go.

Raffaele, sommelier: "I would like my 21 grams to be an aromatic brine, in which I could contain my favorite memories associated with flavors, perfumes, places, people, moments, and music…"

Romina, epicurean: "Perhaps on the day we pass over we can choose what we will become: an animal, a cloud, a sip of espresso, a stain, a shadow, a fingerprint. I would choose a 'sweet-dry-animal' mix made of tonka beans, vetiver, vanilla, and linden flowers wrapped in a orange rose petal in order to remember one of the richest periods of my life."

their authentic charm. Damascus is another capital of the rose. Its perfumers have always been skillful extractors of essences that they used for wall coverings but also to "tint" the house with perfume. It is told that when Saladin conquered Jerusalem, he brought 500 camels laden with rosewater to purify the city before his triumphant entry.

Arabic culture is full of tales of secret gardens burgeoning with flowers. In the first lines of *Sinbad the Sailor* in the *Arabian Nights* we have an exhaustive description: "One day; during the most violent heat of summer, [Sindbad] was carrying a heavy load from one extremity of the city to the other. Much fatigued by the length of the way he had come, he arrived in a street where the pavement was sprinkled with rose-water, and a grateful coolness refreshed the air. Delighted with this mild and pleasant situation, he placed his load on the ground, and took his station near a large mansion. The delicious scent of aloes and frankincense which issued from the windows, the sound of a charming concert issuing from within the house accompanied by the melody of the nightingales, and other birds peculiar to the climate of Bagdad, added to the smell of different sorts of viands, led Sindbad to suppose that some grand feast was in progress. He wished to know to whom this house belonged."

The secret garden is also a recurring theme in design. Le Corbusier designed one on the roof of the Beistegui apartment in Paris in 1930: a room without a ceiling and a lawn in place of a floor, the poetic development of the rooftop garden.

Martha Schwarz's Splice Garden on the roof of the Whitehead Institute in 1997 is almost an homage to Le Corbusier. Irrigation was not possible on the small roof of the building, and so the artist decided to create an ironic work by dividing the garden in half. In one half she created a pop-Zen garden with artificial plants in place of the rocks. In the other half she set up a fake French Renaissance garden also using artificial plants. The scents were left completely to the imagination.

Sulfur

If incense is the aroma of the divine, then sulfur is the exhalation of hell. Tartarus, the underground city of punishment and torment, was a nauseating place, a sinkhole of abominable reeks, but above all a place where olfaction was the means for measuring the crime and applying the punishment. The nose was considered to be a meter for assessing the magnitude of sin. It filtered the mephitic stench of hell which, according to the moral, smelled like a latrine.

In the Christian tradition malodor has always been considered a representation of evil, and the entire literature refers to hell as a poisonous pit, a shadowy foul dungeon to which bodies and souls are condemned. In the *Divina Commedia* [Divine Comedy], Dante Alighieri immerses the simoniacs in excrement, the slothful in the vile reek of the Styx, and he condemns the counterfeiters and alchemists to scabies and leprosy. And Torquato Tasso in the *Gerusalemme Liberata* [Jerusalem Delivered] regarding the mouth of Hades wrote: "So from his mouth flew kindled coals about, hot sparks and smells that man and beast would choke."

Today's cities stink, but no less than their historical forebears, as we may deduce from Süskind's *Perfume*, but the cities standing on volcanoes stink even more because the volcano's vents fill the air with the unmistakable odor of rotten eggs: sulfur. The book *Mediterraneo* by Studio Azzurro describes that "In Naples, as in many cities of the Mediterranean, the soft subsurface is dug out into a labyrinth. You descend into the earth in the center of the city and re-emerge together with the vapors of the many small foundries that have established a habitat there below… In slow motion the incandescent matter is released upwards, transforming the earth into pure vapor. This imaginary cloud moves through the rough cavities of the earth away from the unbearable heat, it spreads out in the cones that naturally aspire upwards towards the yellow sulfur-rimmed orifice, whence it issues forth liberated from the compression and darkness of the grotto. At that point it becomes completely white and rotund and vanishes into the sky."

A project that works along these lines is Vulcania, the European Volcanism Park near

Clermont-Ferrand designed by Hans Hollein in 2002. The center is wholly integrated into the basaltic rock of the landscape, from which it emerges as a regular conical structure faced in basalt. The inside of the cone is covered with golden steel evoking the internal heat of a volcano. Part of the building is dug into the ground, with galleries and rooms that get their light from above, entirely faced in lava slabs and in perfect continuity with their context.

The Place of Fire

Once primitive man grasped the importance of fire the problem became how to bring it inside without burning down the house. So he learned to tame it and keep it alive nourishing it with wood, bushes, and dry grass, which would have released odors that suggested other sapid applications.

The place of fire in architecture is fundamental to understanding the evolution of certain building types. Initially it was near the entrance for reasons that are easy to imagine, and the house was composed of two similar rooms, one for sleeping and the other for daytime activities. The rooms were later diversified as we see in the Greek *megaton* found in Mycenae, comprising a hall and an antechamber. To prevent excessive heat loss, the fire was placed in the center, giving rise to the type of court used in monasteries and European universities. Temperature regulation, and thus the fireplace, had a central position in the dwelling and the smoke was expelled through the roof via a central chimney. But it was an enormous fireplace, as big as a room and as high as a tower, so that everything that needed to be smoke-cured could be hung there. It was not until it was shifted away from the center of the room to one of the walls that it acquired the rectangular form familiar to us today.

When the fires in the house began to multiply and be distributed to two, three, or more points for the various functions – heating (fireplace), cooking (kitchen), lighting (candles, oil lamps) – the modern house was born.

Heating. The Twentieth century architect who dedicated the most energy to thinking about where to put the fire was Frank Lloyd Wright.

61

During the World's Columbian Exposition of 1893 in Chicago he fell in love with Japanese architecture, which he sought to reinterpret throughout his works. An explicit citation was the *tokonoma*, the permanent element in Japanese interiors. It is the center of contemplation and of ceremonies in symbolic and micro-environmental terms, as it would become in many of Wright's houses: the core of the house becomes the fireplace and all the other elements are distributed in relation to this main attractive element.

Cooking. The kitchen also initiated a rationalization phase in those years. Back in the Eighteenth century the introduction of the stove with more than one burner opened the way for new culinary techniques. But it was not until 1869 that a sort of movement was born that studied the management of fire as it related to cooking. This was the year that Catharine Beecher and Harriet Beecher Stowe published their *The American Woman's Home*, partly inspired by the rationalization of galleys on ships. In 1913, Christine Frederick published *The New Housekeeping. Efficiency Studies in Home Management*, which transposed Taylorist labor optimization into the kitchen. In the 1920s the manual arrived in Europe and was translated into many languages. Its translation into architecture is found in the *Siedlungen* [Housing Estates] projects of Ernst May, as part of which Margarete Schütte-Lihotzky would design the famous Frankfurt Kitchen, the prototype of the modern installed kitchen and a sort of *manifesto* regarding rationalization of the domestic environment and its flows, but also a milestone in women's emancipation, not only in the home but also in the field of architecture.

Illuminating. The advent of electricity would slowly displace lighting by oil and wax and thus eliminate their impregnating odors from architecture. It brought eternal day into buildings along with all the ingredients of modern living: air, light, heat.

Nuestra Señora De la Asunción y del Manzano Church, Hondarribia, Basque Country (photo by N. Diaz, 2003)

Per Fumum

In ancient civilizations "perfumes" did not exist in the sense that we know them today. Instead flowers, aromatic plants, and resins were used as offerings to the gods. With time the use of odorous substances intensified and an olfactory aesthetic was born that involved more elaborate products such as suffumigants, oils, balsams, and fermented liquors, all used nevertheless mainly as media for approaching the divine.

None of the great Oriental empires was as religious and at the same time in love with perfumes as ancient Egypt. In the early 2nd millennium BC, the first expedition to modern-day Eritrea resulted in the procurement of incense, myrrh, and the shrubs they were extracted from. Conquests to the east obtained storax, cedar wood, galbanum, and bitumen. The Far East gave them benzoin, cardamom, cinnamon, and pepper. Some of these substances were used in the rituals of reawakening the statue in the morning and others for the rites of unction at the altars.

The original practice of burning the raw materials gave rise to the word "perfume", which derives from the Latin *per fumum* "by means of smoke", through nebulization, the transformation of a substance into something airborne. In ancient times, the methods of perfuming the body were the same as those for perfuming places. Both were accomplished by means of fumigation. "Fumigate" was a synonym for "purify", both in the religious and in the hygienic sense of the word, and this practice soon expanded from the temples into the homes.

Two basic rituals associate scented substances with the worship of gods: fumigation and unction. The burning substances exalted their own odor, rose upwards and were dispersed in the air, reaching all the way to the realm of the divine. The aromatic woods and resins, as well as incense, became the best and most coveted ingredients.

Unction on the other hand involved spreading oil or scented and consecrated paste in certain parts of the sanctuary, on the altars, statues, objects of worship, on the hands and head of the rulers, priests, and the sick, on weapons, on the entrance to houses, and on everything that had to be glorified or protected.

Eventually scented essences were added, including myrrh and spices such as cinnamon or musk, to the mortar during the construction of mosques, so that during the hottest hours of the day, the heat of the sun exalted the perfume and thereby the mystical dimension. The eighty mosques of Harar still give off the scent of myrrh.

Listening to Incens

Incense, or *koh*, was introduced to Japan in the Sixth century by Buddhist monks who used it in their purification rites. It is made from an aromatic wood and became so enrooted in Japanese culture that over the centuries schools were established that taught the art of appreciating it. Incense traces out a continuous thread through the history of Japanese rites and places, including the advent of the industrial era and the way the ancestral rite adapted to it. Such that when Japan participated in the Chicago World's Fair in the late 1800s they presented incense in the form of small cones as we know it today.

And it is only natural that over the centuries a dedicated rite should be developed and elevated to a form of art: *koh-do* or "listening to incense". It is a sort of training in the recognition and taste for this fragrance with very specific rituals similar to the ceremony of tea. Three types of wood are used in the ritual: *Byakudan* (sandalwood), *Jinkoh* (Ginko wood), and *Kyara* (the most valued kind of *jinkoh*, which is more expensive than gold).

Sandalwood is very important because it has well defined applications in architecture: it is strongly scented and resistant to worms and mold; it is a natural bactericide and thus preserves its olfactory properties through time. The sandalwood door to the temple of Somnath was made 2,000 years ago and still emanates its natural scent.

The *koh-do* ceremony takes place in a room in the presence of some fifteen people seated to form a square on the floor. Each player has a sheet of paper on which to record their impressions or observations of each piece of incense presented to them. The *komoto*, the leader of the game or incense presenter, prepares a cup-sized brazier with a hot bamboo coal in a bed

of rice ashes. A small piece of *mica* is placed on the brazier and the incense is placed on the *mica*. The heat causes the wood fragrance to be released to the air without combustion. The *komoto* then takes a couple of inhalations of the incense and passes it to the left with a bow. The person seated to the left of the *komoto* is usually the most honored participant in the ceremony. The cup is passed to the left from person to person, with each of them recording their observations, until it returns to the *komoto*. Each person then interprets their notes, perhaps in the form of a story or poem or as the description of a space.

Tobacco

We live in the full era of prohibition regarding smoking and so entering a house, workplace, public area, or car and smelling cigarette smoke has a strong impact because we are becoming disinured to the presence of this type of smoke in our environment and thus now find it all the more invasive and persistent.

We have returned to the conditions of the time when tobacco was first imported to the West. It was one of the strange and wonderful things brought back by Christopher Columbus, who had found it in Cuba, where the indigenous *tainos* brought to their mouths "firebrands from which they inhaled smoke". Like all invisible things, it was initially considered "the Devil's weed" and condemned by the church and the monarchs. Later it was considered therapeutic and decorative. In the Seventeenth century the Gantiers-Parfumeurs scented it with jasmine, rose, lily of the valley, hyacinth, amber, and musk in accordance with the prevailing tastes of the times.

In the bourgeois households the smoking of cigarettes, cigars, and pipes traced out invisible yet incontestable boundaries between the female quarters and the spaces reserved for men only. The smoking room did not arise for reasons of domestic hygiene, but to create a symbolic masculine space laden with all the misogynistic values of Nineteenth-century bourgeois culture.

There are people and

San Giovanni degli Eremiti, Palermo, Italy (photo by Corbis/Contrasto)

67

places that cannot be imagined without an accompanying odor of smoke, as if this were an integral part of their identity. Places like Cuba or Seville, where the first tobacco processing facilities were founded in 1676, have a history deeply rooted in tobacco and hence their most iconic spots are steeped in its odor.

The architecture typical of the *casas de tabaco* was developed to meet the needs of the production process. It included areas for drying the leaves and for rolling the cigars. Tobacco is cured in large wooden barns with openwork walls to favor natural ventilation. The architecture of cigars and their life cycle and taste are associated with air, sun, humidity, and water.

In order to preserve all of its qualities, each cigar must be stored in conditions mimicking those in the tropical country of its origin. Thus they are kept at a relative humidity of 70% in humidors that breathe, such as cedarwood boxes, that ensure the proper humidity level while allowing the air to circulate. In Geneva, Zino Davidoff revolutionized the cigar trade when he founded Europe's first humidified cigar-storage cellar bringing the ritual of smoking into a similar context as that of wines, and into the world of luxury.

The Tea Ceremony and Coffee Rituals

If we compare what Agatha Christie had to say in *The Mysterious Affair at Styles*, "You will feel better after a piping hot cup of tea, madam", and the words of Edoardo De Filippo in Qu*esti Fantasmi* [These Ghosts], "When I die, bring me a cup of coffee and I will rise from the dead like Lazarus", we may note the profound difference between the world of tea and the world of coffee. The places of tea and coffee are not culturally, geographically, or spatially separated. They are two styles of life that perhaps only now are beginning to be reconciled.

Both are infusions of substances, leaves or seeds that release a very special aroma into the air, the most important sensation of the rite, when they come into contact with heat and steam. The more territorial dimension of these rites is that of the drying of the leaves and the roasting of the coffee beans, which are two processes that release their unmistakable odors into the air and at times serve as landmarks. There are entire regions in India, such as Assam, where tea leaves are dried for the major export brands. And Minas Gerais, Brazil is completely dedicated to coffee cultivation and roasting.

Their pervasive odor and the ritual of their preparation makes them "potions" even before they are beverages. Tea was originally drunk by Zen Buddhist monks, who drank it to remain alert during meditation. Coffee was used in religious rites and for its healing properties. Like all rites both have always had a public and a private dimension composed of irreplaceable places and utensils (teapots and coffee pots) to guarantee the quality of the effect. The tea house and its ceremony are the synthesis of the traditional Japanese architectural module. The tea ceremony (*chado*) is not simply a rite, but a primal matrix of a way of life. *Chado* is carried out in a specially built pavilion in a traditional garden. The pavilion is simply decorated: a vase with flowers, a *kakemono* (a hanging scroll), and the utensils needed for the ceremony.

The protagonist of the rite is *matcha*, the green tea powder onto which boiling water is poured. The infusion is then beaten with a wooden whisk to mix it well but also to spread the vapors in the air. The rite continues with the invitee being served according to a very precise ceremony.

But tea is also a rite that Great Britain exported to its colonies and thus a rite associated with well furnished quarters, aromatic woods, and heavy tapestries. It was a time-odor because it marked the end of the workday as well as social status.

Coffee had a parallel life associated with routes that passed elsewhere but at times crossed those of tea when they were both loaded into the same cargoes on ships and in ports. Originally called "wine of Arabia", it was not until the Fifteenth century that it gained such status as a symbol of conviviality that two cafés were opened in Istanbul. The Catholic church kept it away from the Sacred Empire because it was "too Islamic". And so it was not until the Seventeenth century that coffee began to be imported to Venice from Cairo. The passion for coffee then spread into central Europe, and from there to France and to the rest of the world.

It became a dual-component rite. There was brewed coffee served in large cups and generally accompanied by pastries, and in 1822 the first espresso machine was made which would later become the driving force behind the burgeoning success of Italian-style cafés. Cafés became important places in Europe, showcases for politics, culture, and lifestyle. Cities like Vienna became capitals of cafés and even the architect Adolf Loos designed one in 1899: the Cafe Museum.

Religion by Erminia De Luca, 2005

MARKETING
AND TIME

Conservation and Acceleration

Salvador Dalí said that of the five human senses, the sense of smell is the one that best renders the idea of immortality. Perhaps he wanted to emphasize the vocation of olfaction for manipulating the time that measures out the lifespan of an odor, but which is also its greatest enemy. The temporal cycle of an odor can follow a natural rhythm, or else it can be planned, accelerating or decelerating the processes of transformation and aging, and thus altering its duration.

The fact that time and the sense of smell are connected is also affirmed by Marshall McLuhan in *Understanding Media: The Extensions of Man*, where he writes that both the Chinese and the Japanese up to the Seventeenth century measured time by gradations of incense; they measured hours and days, and also seasons by a careful sequence of scents. The three elements that characterize the duration of an odor (top, middle, and bottom) have different timeframes, intensities, and qualities. Planning the duration of an odor is something of great interest in both marketing and art, but

for different reasons. Both seek to enhance or exaggerate the performance of the product, but they develop the relationship between space and olfaction in two different ways: one seeks to separate cause and effect, using odors as an end rather than a vehicle for experience; the other seeks to recover, a bit philologically, the odors of materials, bodies, and spaces, and often makes them into exhibition pieces.

The identity of a place is determined partly by its odors. If this identity is not particularly meaningful one can be invented or bought. In this sense there are two works of art, both working with natural elements, that render the idea of the processes of acceleration and conservation: the *Earth Room III* by Walter De Maria (the first installation dates back to 1977) currently installed in a New York gallery, and the installation by Zaha Hadid and Cai Guo-Qiang for the *Snow Show* in Rovaniemi in 2004.

Walter De Maria's third work in the series, *Earth Room*, is a room full of loose, odorous soil, kept

Exhibition with the air – Genoa – (photo by R. Monzini, 2004)

moist by a system that controls the relative humidity. The sensation of humidity and conservation is profound. The spectator seems to breathe an eternal, ancestral experience, the same emotion one might have in front of something that has always been there, even though it is clear that this is not the case here. The constructions by Hadid and Guo-Qiang for the *Snow Show* in Rovaniemi, Finland consisted of two mirroring landscape formations, one made of ice and the other of snow. At a certain point, the Chinese artist sprinkled vodka on the snow structure and set it alight, causing the snow to liquefy and initiating movements of water, fire, and air. The lines of fire sculpted the forms, softening the corners and creating a constantly mutating profile. All was quickly consumed, the architecture as well, in a sort of fast-motion movie.

Greenhouses

The 1800s was the century when the hygienists sought to appropriate and recover architectural spaces, where odor was considered to be a synonym for unhealthiness and filth. It began with the World's Fairs that would be the first true exercise of glass and steel industrial architecture. There were no ready-made models, and so the architects borrowed them from other realms: railway stations, bridges, greenhouses, with this last category becoming the model for the pavilions at the international fairs.

In Alessandro Baricco's novel *Oceano Mare* [Ocean Sea] there is a very vivid rendition of the Crystal Palace, described as an enormous greenhouse with only three gigantic elms inside. But he invites the reader to imagine it with thousands of people inside, with all its fixtures and objects brought in from all over the world. And he also invites us to step into other realms of perception and imagine all the sounds and voices, and the plethora of odors.

And what indeed are greenhouses if not enormous glass ampoules in which scented flowers and plants grow? The Nineteenth century was marked by the emergence of mass production, of industrial processes, of the first synthetic products. In architecture and perfumery the attempt was made to associate natural components with synthetic products and advanced materials. Nevertheless it took some time for the engineers to achieve architectural elegance and for the alchemists to achieve the refinement of modern perfumes.

There are numerous ampoule-like buildings. One of the pioneer projects was Buckminster Fuller's Dymaxion House (1945), a prototype energy-efficient house that never went into production. It is part of the permanent exhibits at the Henry Ford Museum in Dearborn, Michigan. It was a spherical structure similar to the bell of a jellyfish. There was a nebulizer-shower to minimize water consumption and the entire dome of the house could rotate to take advantage of the wind for natural air conditioning.

One of the most extraordinary projects along these lines is the Eden Project of 2001 by Nicholas Grimshaw & Partners in Cornwall. The skin of the building, a sort of second sky, encloses a microcosm, and its lightness counteracts the dizzying immensity of the self-supporting domes, up to 124 meters in diameter. They are triple-skinned geodetic domes. The skins are made of ETFE (Ethylene Tetra Fluoro Ethylene Co-Polymer) pillows inflated by compressors. The weight of the entire construction is less than that of the air contained within it. The greenhouse contains not only exotic plants, but also more common species such as hot pepper, tobacco, cotton, tea, and coffee.

There is another greenhouse that will be built in San Francisco, the world capital of environmentalism, by the Renzo Piano Building Workshop, as an annex to the California Academy of Sciences. It will take the place of the current pavilions that have been there since 1916 and will be characterized by a large rectangular roof with soft undulations in elevation. The roof will be almost completely covered with vegetation except for some glass portions. The building will be an efficient, integrated active/passive thermal engine. The most significant innovative design aspect is the natural "chimney effect" ventilation system, which captures the humid and temperate sea wind to cool the facility in the summer and supplements the heating system in the winter. The air

A tour of Parma, City of Perfume by Nicola Pozzani

We start on the banks of the Parma river where the famous Parma violet grows, a flower that has lent its fragrance to places and customs. First among these are those initiated by the duchess Maria Luigia. The beloved queen founded a sort of cult for the violet that would soon spread outside the bounds of the city, creating a style that connoted good taste and refinement. She left a bountiful legacy of her noble game of love (much of which is found in the city's Napoleonic Museum): toiletry sets, fans, dishes, paintings, thimbles, diaries, letter paper, bottles of perfume, as well as a botanical garden.

The city's flower was adopted by the most fashion-conscious as well: violets in hairdos, in gloves, on silk handkerchiefs, even at the theater or cinema which were outfitted with perfume sprayers. The Parma violet completed and embellished a style, officially called 'Liberty', which gave it a formal and visual expression.

The success of this essence and its innumerable composed fragrances started in a specific place, the barber shop, where perfumes were used to embellish the service. Given the presence in Parma of complementary sectors such as glass-working, fashion and leather goods, and illustration, it was not long before perfumes gave birth to a full blown industry. Experiments were carried out in perfumed printed works for a famous illustrated barber's calendar. It resonated internationally and an "olfactory district" near the train station strategically sealed the vocation of that market. Memories of this scenario can be breathed at the Museo del Profumo in the Palazzina Borsari, the historic Parmesan perfumery.

It would be difficult to imagine the history of that once tiny provincial capital without perfume adding cheer to its spaces, without the emotional fragrance of a coquettish scenario of pleasure.

enters via intakes on the south wall, warms up thanks to the greenhouse effect, and is extracted and delivered to the exhibition area through mobile ports in the roof. The power will derive substantially from the acceleration of air near the exits. The building will be partially powered by photovoltaic cells on the south-facing surfaces, while water management will be accomplished using sea pressure to fill underground tanks that will regulate the temperature of the floor.

The Genie of the Lamp

Scents and cosmetics are two tightly wedded realms, not only for the characteristics of their ingredients and products, but especially because they share the same aspirations and vocations. A perfume in a bottle may be considered a genie in a magic lamp because its mission is to be a vehicle for desire, pleasure, seduction, memory, getting closer, holding on, loving, and power, as if the perfume emerges in its ethereal, genie-like form when you open the bottle and grants your any wish.

There is a passage in the *Arabian Nights* where the genie is described in a way similar to a perfume: "He examined the jar on all sides; he shook it to see if it would rattle. But he heard nothing, and so, judging from the impression of the seal and the lid, he thought there must be something precious inside. To find out, he took his knife, and with a little trouble he opened it. He turned it upside down, but nothing came out, which surprised him very much. He set it in front of him, and whilst he was looking at it attentively, such a thick smoke came out that he had to step back a pace or two. This smoke rose up to the clouds, and stretching over the sea and the shore, formed a thick mist, which caused the fisherman much astonishment. When all the smoke was out of the jar it gathered itself together, and became a thick mass in which appeared a Genie, twice as large as the largest giant."

Boullée's cenotaph was never built, but the sensation it would certainly have generated is that of finding oneself in a huge perfume bottle, in an air bubble with a utopian scent. The tangible sensation of an air bubble is found in a number of installations of the Argentinean artist Tomas Saraceno, who in 2005 installed his *In-form the air: Air Under Different Pressure* in an art gallery in Genoa. A transparent PVC membrane was filled with air to create a giant bubble six meters high that adhered to the walls of the room and left an air space above at a different pressure that allowed visitors to "stroll" upon the bubble. The air pressure inside the bubble was higher so that you could feel it in your eardrums but was not particularly bothersome. The visitors suspended on top of the bubble looked like figures in relief on a Seventeenth century ceiling. The pressure of their bodies on the membrane caused the air to circulate inside the bubble. These installations are temporary architectures that introduce the body into the ampoule as an ingredient of the magic.

Martin Ruiz de Azúa's *Basic House* (1999) comprises a one-person bubble coated with PVC film that expands under the heat of the sun. Certain performances of the contemporary artist Victorine Müller involve the artist herself or other people inside inflatable ampoules as in *Gate C* (2003) and *Timeline* (2005). During the seventies, in Superstudio's *Città delle Semisfere*, 10,044,900 sarcophaguses made of transparent material contained motionless individuals with their eyes closed who breathe constantly replenished conditioned air and are nourished directly via their blood.

Vacuum Packed

Unlike wine, perfume does not improve with age. Instead, it changes, degrades, becomes denatured, and evaporates. However there are a number of devices used to preserve it. Light, heat, and humidity are its worst enemies, oxidizing or otherwise breaking down the fragile perfume molecules. It has to be shielded from ultraviolet rays and protected against evaporation. It should be isolated from other materials and surfaces to prevent bacterial contamination and degradation. Coolness and darkness are excellent allies for preserving scents, but subzero temperatures and vacuums are even better. Once again, the ancient Egyptians were the precursors. You could consider the pyramids as a structure where the door was a filling port rather than an entryway.

Storing things in a vacuum is not just a technique for preserving them in time. It is also hygienic and an excellent means for maintaining the organoleptic qualities of the product, whatever it may be. This is the sense of Marcel Duchamp's 1919 work *Air de Paris* [Air of Paris], a glass test tube filled with "authentic Parisian air". It was one of his ready-mades and a souvenir that Duchamp gave as a gift to his friend Walter Arensberg. Using the same concept in 1961, Piero Manzoni created *Fiato d'artista* [Artist's Breath], a series of 45 "air bodies" that were nothing more than balloons inflated with the artist's own breath.

The Medium is the Message

With this famous phrase from sixties Pop Art, Marshall McLuhan affirmed that there is no message other than the medium. Communication by means of perfumes has always followed this orientation. Fashion and perfumery have always shared the same aesthetic dictates. There is an immense literature dedicated to perfumes, especially to fine fragrances, which explains above all why, starting at a certain point in the 1900s, stylists decided to dress us not only in their clothing creations, but also in fragrances. But the practice of wearing scented objects and perfumes to extend one's aura beyond one's physical body has always existed.

During the era of the ancient Egyptian New Kingdom (1570-1085 BC) guests attending celebrations placed cones of myrrh or animal fat in their headdresses in order to create an invisible aura that enhanced their charisma.

The Romans were also maniacs regarding the use of perfumes on their bodies, in their homes, and in association with events. Nero was so thoroughly seduced by this world that he was completely intemperate in his use of scents. There were celebrations where rose petals were suspended from the ceiling in nets which were opened to deluge the guests with a scented "rain", at times actually suffocating them. In the Imperial age rose petals were scattered on the seats at the circuses, and the spectators were sprayed with scented essences. Things reached a peak of excess with Heliogabalus. It is said that one of the determining factors in the final collapse of the Roman Empire was the depletion of the state treasury by the heavy costs of importing incense and perfume.

The Oriental and Arab worlds were always familiar with perfumes, which reached the Occident with the return of the Crusaders and first entered the market via the trading networks of the seaboard republics: Pisa, Amalfi, Genoa, and Venice.

In that period one of the most important perfumes was dried myrtle leaves, an especially strategic article because it also was used in leather tanning. One of the modern world's perfume capitals, Grasse, began its history in scents with trade in myrtle leaves, which were also used in the flourishing local tanning industry. Florence has a similar history in this regard. Towards the end of the Eleventh century the Crusaders brought back rosewater, musk, and amber, substances that were banned by the Catholic church until the Seventeenth century when a Franciscan friar, Domenico Auda, began to market a sacred-profane water for churches and the dwellings of nobles. It was a sort of perfume to adorn homes and churches with the same beatifying scent.

It was in the Eighteenth century that perfume regained its status as an unparalleled aesthetic expression; perfume corrected ugliness, exalted appearance over reality, adorned the body, and decorated spaces. The apotheosis of this aesthetic of illusion was the court of Louis XV in France, also known as the "perfumed court", where it was actually obligatory to use a different perfume every day.

Hygiene was rediscovered and the more evolved tastes appreciated the more delicate perfumes that made the fortune of the first grand Parisian *maisons*. The chemists in Grasse prospered and enormously improved the techniques of *enfleurage* and distillation. In Cologne, Jean-Antoine Farina introduced the first Eau de Cologne.

There were two scents that marked the end of the Monarchy and the beginning of the French Revolution. One was the perfume worn by Marie Antoinette, who, as leg-

Crystal Palace by Joseph Paxton, London, 1851

end has it, was betrayed by its unmistakable bouquet as she was trying to flee. The other is the odor of gunpowder which pervaded the streets of Paris during the armed clashes.

Strongly associated with the profligacy of the court, perfumes disappeared for a period until they returned to favor under the Consulate and the Napoleonic Empire. The Empress Josephine squandered a fortune on exotic perfumes and Napoleon was exaggeratedly fond of his Eau de Cologne rub-downs.

English empiricism also played a role in establishing the importance of the sense of smell and the senses generally. It is a philosophy that sees the senses as being the source of all knowledge. Starting from the idea that the basis of all knowledge is experience, many scholars began to use their senses, the sense of smell included, more intensively.

In the 1800s the perfume industry grew exponentially, accompanied by a spread of the use of perfume among all social classes and the establishment of the hygienist theories, which led people to begin frequenting the seaside and spas. The "vaporizer" made its appearance at the 1868 Paris World's Fair and quickly consigned all other ways of applying perfume to oblivion. But it also marked the passing of the traditional, artisanal stage. New discoveries in the chemistry of fragrances and aromas, and developments in the corresponding industry generated new needs and thus new products and olfactory delights.

Scents became the masks of the bourgeois ego. Perfumes were worn for exalting special occasions and not for therapeutic purposes. Perfumes became definitively separated from pharmaceuticals and established themselves as fully fledged cosmetic brands.

An extremely interesting period in the relation between perfumery, architecture, and design came at the end of the First World War, when Europe seemed to be imbued with winds of creativity and optimism. Black Art took center stage at the Exposition of Decorative Arts in Paris in 1925. The Cubists gained acclaim, and a passion for Japan spread through the avant-garde movements. These were the years in which Coco Chanel revolutionized the image of women and, in opposition to overly sweet scents and white flowers, she launched one of perfume's greatest icons, *Chanel no. 5*, which is still an international top seller. For the first time a fashion house created its own line of perfumes and in a matter of just a few years some of the most incredible perfumes of the Twentieth century were born: *Shalimar*, *Joy*, and *Arpege*.

Travel and Trade

Perfumes and trade in their raw materials have often been the driving forces behind travel, commerce, and great discoveries. People have always come back from their travels bringing with them the odors of the places they have visited. We have an extraordinary capacity to associate an experience abroad with one or more odors. Perhaps in unfamiliar places our sensorial "compasses" are especially sensitive, or this may be simply because we are more relaxed. What is certain is that every destination is associated in our memory with a very specific olfactory "postcard" that is more indelible than our visual memories.

Five or six thousand years ago there were already many civilizations who used perfumes: the Egyptians along the Nile, the Cretans, the civilizations along the Tigris and Euphrates, those on the Yellow River or the Indus, and those on the shores of the Baltic sea. But the first city to combine trade in aromatic plants, perfume production, and the manufacture of perfume bottles was Corinth.

The Orient was the world's largest market for perfume ingredients, which were grown locally or imported from distant lands. Trade in these materials contributed to the prosperity of the Phoenicians, and to the foundation of Palmyra, Petra, and Antioch. Incense powered the establishment of the kingdoms of Arabia, whose immense wealth survives through the legend of the Queen of Sheba.

There is an invisible thread linking odors to the histories of a series of cities over the centuries: Corinth in the Sixth century; Constantinople in the Middle Ages until it was conquered by the Ottomans in 1453; Venice, where the alembic was perfected and modern perfumery was born; and then France, with Grasse being the center of production and Paris the center of distribution.

The role of travelers was thus fundamental in the intermixing of olfactory ingredients from all over the world. Marco Polo came back from his expeditions with perfumes and spices, described in *Il Milione* [The Travels of Marco Polo], that ensured Venice a monopoly in perfume markets in the Middle Ages. While the routes to the Orient were opened by the likes of Polo, Christopher Columbus was the pioneer of the westward explorations, bringing home hitherto unknown ingredients such as vanilla, tobacco, and cardamom.

Physiological Architecture

The term "physiological architecture" was coined by Philippe Rahm and Jean-Gilles Décosterd to describe their approach to architecture, which deals with the interactions that the space outside of the body can produce within the body. Their work concentrates on the possibility of affecting physiological states through architecture, and thus on the ways of inhabiting architectural spaces.

Beyond the sensory perception of spatial agents within the realm of our five recognized senses, there are also other receptors that produce neither sensations, nor perceptions, but that nevertheless alter the state of the subject. These include photosensitive skin cells, receptors associated with the retina sending signals directly to the epithalamic and hypothalamic system, humidity receptors in the upper respiratory tract, and vomeronasal receptors of volatile emanations such as pheromones.

Physiological architecture is noteworthy not just for the reactions it provokes, but for its almost complete absence of structure, of a building. What occurs in their works is the clear manifestation of what normally occurs in people, but raised to an extra-corporeal dimension: breathing in the Hormonorium; sleeping in the Melatonin Room; and sweating in the Omnisports Room.

The Hormonorium was set up in the Swiss Pavilion at the 2003 Venice Biennale, reproducing the sensation of high altitude: of hypo-oxygenation and lighting from below. The floor was a blindingly luminous platform made of Plexiglas that lets UV rays pass through from 528 fluorescent tubes emitting a white light that mimics the solar spectrum. Light coming from below is not filtered by the eyelashes. It strikes the retina, which sends signals to the pineal gland causing melatonin production to drop. The decrease in this hormone results in diminished fatigue and increased sexual desire. Air is the other fundamental component of the installation. It is enriched with nitrogen, causing a reduction in the relative amount of oxygen and thus mimicking high altitude air. This slight hypoxia causes some initial disorientation as well as a faint euphoria induced by the production of endomorphine. The end result is a sort of 'doping' effect that results in roughly a 10% increase in physical performance.

Another project is the *Jardins physiologiques* that explores the idea of creating an intra–corporeal landscape architecture that interacts with and unsettles our own internal garden by means of our senses and our brains' hormonal and thymic systems. The project takes the visitor through four "gardens" relating to different dimensions of perception. The first is tactile where the experience ranges from extreme softness to extreme prickliness. Then there is a garden of the nose, with everything from the sweetest to the most nauseating scents. The garden of taste encompasses the most delicious and the most disgusting flavors. The last garden takes visitors through the states of the mind, from the most soothing to the most distressing.

Subliminal

In Süskind's *Perfume* there is an exhaustive description of why odors are both wonderful and terrible at the same time:

"People could close their eyes to greatness, to horrors, to beauty, and their ears to melodies or deceiving words. But they could not escape scent. For scent was a brother of breath. Together with breath it entered human beings, who could not defend themselves against it, not if they wanted to live. And scent entered into their very core, went directly to their hearts, and decided for good and all between affection and contempt, disgust and lust, love and hate. He who ruled scent ruled the hearts of men."

It is precisely this hidden but powerful domain, this inexorable power over emotions, that makes odors both attractive and dangerous.

Air Pandan by Nancy Martin

Like Cole Porter's lady who gets no kick from champagne, I get no kick from perfume. I get my kicks from smells, raw smells that suddenly invade and occupy my private space, smells everybody likes like fresh coffee, snow air and the smell it deposits on the laundry, raindrops on hot dry earth and more personal smells like the mix of stale cigarette smoke and light perspiration of my friend's jacket. Smells that come up on you suddenly when you least expect it and take you away to somewhere you have been before, something that happened, or someone you once knew. To get the kick, all this must happen by chance.

On my last trip to Parma I ran into a smell. I just missed the bus and I had an hour to wait. Instead of the little 50's bar I usually go to, I decided to check out a new shop a few doors up. A Chinese shop, totally out of place in the land of culatello and tortellini. The shop has no name and the windows are packed hodge-podge with little tea sets and dusty plastic toys and cans of mysterious foodstuffs, so that you could not see anything of the inside. I opened the door to bump into a group of Africans at the checkout counter just after a display case of Chinese medicines and cosmetics, fake hairpieces and little bottles. There was just enough space for one person in the aisles loaded with merchandise - on the shelves, on the floor, every-where stuff piled up. Nothing excites me more than this kind of shop, where you can gaze at the unknown for hours for the price of a can of coconut milk or a piece of tofu, or a handful of bright green peperonci-ni. A world in itself.

Impossible to undertake a thorough inspection of this shop - it would take hours and I had only one. My senses in overdrive, I picked my way through the aisles cluttered with packages and an occasional cus-tomer to the food area. And there it was. A row of neat glass bottles - the top covered with white paper and labelled Air Pandan. I am back in Bali. I am at the Denpasar market, under the stairway to the lower level where they sell food and flower offerings. I am in the corner where the ladies sell Balinese sweets. I smell my favourite, a set of five small white balls of sticky rice on a little tray made from a folded banana leaf. When you break the sticky rice ball sweet palm sugar is squirted onto your tongue. The sweet is per-fumed with Air Pandan.

Useless to describe the sensation, it is an experience everyone has sometime. Air Pandan is the essence of a homely plant that looks like the aloes cactus. It has long thin leaves the Balinese shred into tiny fila-ments and put into their daily offerings to the multitude of divinities they feed every day. For the people down here on earth like me, Air Pandan is a whiff of paradise. I have been thinking these past few days that I must go back again to the Chinese food shop. As soon as possible.

Modifying the odor of something means having an impact on the emotional sphere that drives our choices. For this reason the olfactory realm is the last frontier for marketing, communication, and art.

A Westerner entering a space and smelling lavender will immediately have the feeling that it is an aerated and clean place, even if it is actually enclosed and dirty. This exemplifies how the sense of smell can be much more powerful than sight. Here, even if our sense of smell is in conflict with what we see, we instinctively put more credence in what we smell. If, by some strange caprice of the air currents, the odor of boiled cabbage should make its way into a Gothic cathedral, the image of the place in the eyes – or nose – of the beholder will be drastically altered – and good-bye aura of mystic asceticism! We trust our noses more than our eyes. It is no fluke that many expression for communicating trust or distrust use olfactory metaphors.

Emotional Marketing

When Heraclites wrote "if all things were smoke the nose would recognize them", he was either expressing a comforting truth or unacceptable ingenuousness. In any case we can never overstate the fact that the sense of smell is both the most authentic and the most adulterated of our senses.

In the generalized system of creating copies and surrogates for reality, olfaction is one of the major accomplices in making the false seem true, for increasing the apparent realism of an experience that would otherwise be evanescent, and for supporting commercial, environmental, and artistic metaphors with sensory experience.

If artistic expressions where the senses are the media for giving the work unity and coherence are termed "sensorial", then artistic expressions where the senses are the goal of the work may be termed "sensorialisms". When Brian Eno composed *Music for Airports* in the late seventies, the boundary line between the artist's attempt to forge into new territories and a bald-faced commercial pursuit was not clear. When the phenomenon later became truly commercial with Muzak, piped into offices and stores in Japan and the United States, many were sarcastically perplexed.

And yet in the following years the soundscape became more and more a part of our lives, expanding the range of emotional and psychological states that a place is "allowed" to arouse in us without it being looked at with suspicious or irritation. For a number of years now the same thing has been happening in the field of artificial deodorization of spaces. In absolute and also justified emulation of their auditory counterparts one now speaks of made-to-order "olfactory landscapes". These are usually found in places that have no identity in the olfactory sense. They are not "non-places" as Marc Augé would define them, but places with little personality.

In effect, these are the places best suited to new odors, because their lack of particular olfactory characteristics makes it possible to design new odors without having to rid the space of pre-existing ones. Having determined that odor can communicate and exalt the experience of a place and enhance its memorableness – as already occurs for extraordinary experiences, such as a vacation or a lovers' tryst – our extremely consumption-oriented society seeks to make even the most normal experiences "extraordinary", increasing their real impact, perhaps via their olfactory dimension.

In Marco Polo's times the Chinese used to perfume their fabrics with patchouli leaves and vetiver roots in order to inspire in their customers a desire to buy. Nowadays a similar thing happens with cars, restaurants, hotels, and shopping centers, as well as in workplaces in order to increase worker productivity. In London's Heathrow Airport the scent of pine is released into the air in order to put people at ease. Many Japanese companies actually use different odors over the course of the day to stimulate and enhance work: a bit of lemon in the early morning, flowers a little later, and forest scents in the early afternoon.

In shopping malls and commercial spaces scents are used to induce customers to linger, to tone down their aggressive impulses, to induce the desire to buy, or to make an outrageously high price seem justifiable. In his book *Parallax*, Steven Holl writes about such a place: "My recent stay at a Ramada Inn in the Midwest began in a lobby with no natural light (blank walls to a parking lot), which lead to a confusing series of Sheetrock-lined, carpeted, double-loaded corridors that smelled of perfumed cleaning fluid. Finally, the wood-grained Formica door opened to a polyester-carpeted 'large room' with vinyl wallpaper and an acoustic-panel ceiling. Though the smell was stifling, the anodized aluminum window was not operable. Synthetic (and sometimes toxic) interiors of typical lodgings scattered in polluted landscapes characterize today's throw-away environment."

Removal

In *The Nose* in Nikolai Gogol's *St. Petersburg Novels*, the protagonist wakes up one morning without a nose. "My God, my God! Why has this misfortune come upon me? Even loss of hands or feet would have been better, for a man without a nose is the devil knows what — a bird, but not a bird, a citizen, but not a citizen, a thing just to be thrown out of window. It would have been better, too, to have had my nose cut off in action, or in a duel, or through my own act: whereas here is the nose gone with nothing to show for it — uselessly — for not a groat's profit!''.

Designing with scents does not mean simply deodorizing spaces, but quite often means purifying the air of existing odors and then perhaps reodorizing the spaces. The housing products industry has been oriented for decades towards products that cover up household odors, with no strategy regarding their elimination. It is certainly more difficult to eliminate an odor than it is to produce one or release it into the air. Ridding a space of odors requires such things as ventilation, air filtering, etc. One chemically-based process that is certainly very effective for purifying the air of odors is oxidation using hydrogen peroxide. There are also filters, as in the Japanese product *Black Cube*, based on silica gel, aluminum hydroxide, and kaolin. One disadvantage of these approaches is that they work indiscriminately to remove both unpleasant and desirable odors.

Other substances that purify the air include

chlorine – which does in fact remove all odors but leaves you literally unable to breathe – and activated carbon, which is used in olfactometers and in air purification filters. An installation along these lines is *La Camera Linda* [The Clean Room] (1986) by Clino Trini Castelli and Marek Piotrowski. It introduced a special technical chamber, known as the *camera bianca* [white room], into the domestic environment. This sort of room is normally what is used to protect highly sophisticated equipment (as in computer rooms or control rooms). The air treatment affected the non-material components but also the emotional reactions of visitors who were disoriented by finding themselves in a domestic setting with the sort of aseptic air typical of technological environments.

This brings to mind when Italo Calvino, in *Sotto il Sole Giaguaro* [Under the Jaguar Sun], states: "Epigraphs in an undecipherable language, half their letters rubbed away by the sand-laden wind: this is what you will be, *O parfumeries*, for the noseless man of the future."

Placebo

It has been asserted that perfumes produce a placebo effect.

Paracelsus was the first to suggest that perfumes might be closely in tune with the human spirit, that they could give places a magnetism, they could excite, depress, facilitate intuition, etc. On a number of occasions in history perfumes have been used as placebos, innocuous substances having the purpose of calming, soothing, and healing. During the bombing of London in the Second World War, the British sprayed lavender in their bomb shelters, not just to cover up unpleasant odors, but perhaps more so to calm their fears. The scent of lavender evoked for them a clean and reassuring home-like setting, the exact opposite of their actual situation.

Odor is a vehicle for rendering an experience more enveloping and memorable. It both reinforces the experience and can also make an illusory experience verisimilar. The scent of coconut oil may give someone the impression that they are on vacation in the heat of the Maldives rather than on a lunch break in a freezing metropolis.

93

With the high social value placed on health and showing it off, other types of placebo-places are very popular, such as the oxygen bars. The principle is both simple and perverse: you go to a bar to inhale oxygen scented with mint, eucalyptus, sage and basil, lemon, or ylang ylang. The idea is to "pretend to be healthy" because the time actually spent inhaling, about 10 minutes, is not enough to clean the smog out of the lungs. However, the placebo effect is certainly achieved.

One of the stranger works by Philippe Rahm and Jean-Gilles Décosterd is *Peinture Placebo*©, which is a way of "hoodwinking" the subject. It has been observed that the placebo effect triggers the release of dopamine (the neurotransmitter involved with satisfaction of desires and the generation of a sense of pleasure), which affects the brain's motivation and rewards system. *Peinture Placebo*© was presented in an exhibition at the Paris Musée d'Art Moderne and involved mixing into otherwise perfectly normal industrial white paint an infinitesimal dose of ginger or orange blossoms. Visitors were asked to specify the purpose or nature of the room without recourse to visual representations. The effect was such that the orange blossom room was considered relaxing and the ginger room charged with eroticism. Although the cause was a placebo, the resulting effect certainly was not.

Art
by Erminia De
Luca, 2005

LES ATELIERS HERMÈS, PARIS – It is the center of production for the French manufacturer of luxury leather goods. Founded as a saddle making company in 1837, Hermès now creates accessories, clothing and perfume. The site was designed by Constantin Voyatzis and Rena Dumas with the idea of visible work, like a beehive or a Moroccan medina. Leatherworkers in the atelier handcraft each item from beginning to end, individually involved in all phases of sewing, embossing, waxing, assembly and finishing. Much of the creation is done without machinery and in certain ateliers the only sounds are of metal hand tools on leather. There are six ateliers on the premises, each with about thirty workers.

HERVÉ ELLENA – He is a Paris based architect. His latest design was for the rehabilitation and extension of the *Institut de France* in Paris, and numerous projects for highway structures across France.

JEAN-CLAUDE ELLENA – He is Hermès' in-house perfumer since 2004. Some of his previous major creations are *First* for Van Cleef & Arpels, three fragrances for Frederic Malle and Bulgari's *Eau de Thé Vert.* He has created two Hermès fragrances inspired by the garden: *Un Jardin en Méditerranée* and *Un Jardin sur le Nil,* and a collection called *Hermessence.* In 2006, he created the house's new masculine fragrance: *Terre d'Hermès.*

HE – In architecture perfume is almost never thought about. Olfaction is related to the dark side of architecture, in what people forget to plan, and in the details that are overlooked when we think of how one lives in a place. Often these are the things that come about unconsciously. They are not in the plans or the details, but you feel them when you build and on the construction site. Mostly it's intuition. Anyway, I'm aware of the smell of the building materials that I use, like wood, but maybe it's because I have this family history.

JCE – Architecture is the art of space and to measure the quality of a perfume, you measure its efficiency in space. When someone wears a perfume, you don't have to get close to smell it as the perfume occupies a space. This space is important in the expression of the perfume; the perfume is also an expression of the space. The first smell you have around here, as you enter this space, is leather. It's subtle - it comes from those armchairs over there - but it's present and Hermès is leather oriented, their work is about leather. When you create a perfume there is a way to structure a *formula*; you have components that structure the smell. Components are ornaments, details. You play with these ornaments and the structure; sometimes ornaments can become structure and sometimes structure can become an ornament. In this way there is a link with architecture. You can invent new structure all the time because the way to think in perfumery today is not to take a structure from the past, but to invent a new structure.

In perfumery it takes five to ten years to be able to use a new element, to understand how to handle it. When a new material arrives everyone is scared by it, but step by step they find a way how to use it. But it's not like a new molecule arrives and one makes a new perfume. This is bullshit! *[Laughs]* This is marketing talk. Aldehydes were invented in 1904 and people started using them. In 1921, the invention of *Chanel No.5* got people talking about aldehydes, but in fact they were being used for almost twenty years. Don't reduce perfumery to one new molecule, because you can take away this molecule and the fragrance will almost be the same. It's *Chanel No.5* that made aldehydes, and not the aldehydes that made *Chanel No.5*.

HE – There's the same example in architecture: reinforced concrete was invented by a French, Joseph-Louis Lambot, and the first things he made with it were flower pots and even small boats. He conceived of things and made them at his scale, taking steel and shaping concrete around it. But it took time to have real expression with concrete, to adapt it and imagine what could be done with it. The final use of a material is perhaps different from how it was originally conceived. The first use of new materials, even new techniques in architecture, is often ornament.

JCE – It always takes a long time to adapt and to invent *the* way for a new material to be part of the story. I look at all the new materials, some I reject, others I keep, and out of my selection, perhaps there is a product that I will use in two, three or four years. I know they are there and when I have a new idea for a perfume, I remember one and say: "Oh, yes, this could be part of my story."

HE – It takes time to understand how to use simple things as well. I build mostly in wood and it took me time to understand how it works and not to just put things on top of each other. But it is not written, you have to find a way through each material.

JCE – The smell here is, of course, of leather, different kinds of leather; but there is also the smell of glue. All leathers have different smells, some are flowery, some are woody, others smell of varnish. It depends on the leather and the way they prepare it. Goat leather doesn't have the same smell as calfskin. I'm working on a series of perfumes based on leather, but I'm really taking my time because I want them to be right. The people working here must get so used to the leather smell that they don't notice it anymore. But if somehow the place's odor was removed, the people would say: "This is not our place."
So the olfactory information is still there, even if they're used to it.

HE – I worked in a perfume factory when I was very young and I noticed that it always had the same smell. The products would change - one day shampoo, another day perfume - but in the end the smell was always

the same; it's called *mille fleurs*. I would get so used to the smell that I didn't notice it, but if I came from the factory and didn't take a shower, my friends would say: "Oh, you smell of *cocotte!*"

HE – Here it smells of ironing, like in a laundry.

JCE – Here the odor is very different than the smell of the bag atelier, which smelled strongly of leather. Instead here it smells of hot iron.

HE – You can see in the ateliers here that everyone takes care in the way that the bags in progress are posed very neatly, and the way their tools are placed around them, but never in the same way. This is a part of architecture that no one sees. No one should think about this before workers arrive. You have to make the space as open as possible.

Here some tools or cabinets have no real place, they occupy unused space, it seems as if they could not find a natural place - or maybe this very place was lacking this "naturalness."

This is a permanent issue in architecture – we should think about most things, but not too much, because we don't know how the people are going to work. Even if we wanted to know how they work, we would be wrong. We must have some intuition about how people works in order to draw plans - to have an idea of the size, shape and scale of the place - but not to predetermine the placement of every object, because that never works.

When you build something you change the surroundings. But the surroundings change the architecture in return. This is true at all scales.

When I've built things in the countryside, in the center of France, it was mostly for programs for buildings for taking care of roads - garages, offices for highway maintenance. In these cases the primal architectural concern was the topography of the land, and wind direction. This meant getting in the right direction for the wind, because if you have a big garage with five meters by five meters doors, too much wind will float the doors off.

At the same time we thought about landscapes and vistas, the upcoming users as well, but once you've dealt with the engineering issue, then you can explore a range of questions: if you want to bury the building in the hill, or on the contrary, to overexposed it, and so on. The questioning stops only when the architect feels a resolution to the questions that have been posed. Architecture is over concerned with how the building will be seen. If it's near a highway you might think you'll see the building only from the point of view of the traffic. Often a problem with builders and construction firms is that they say: "No one will ever see this, so why care?" Architects must always fight, to say that the unseen is as important as the seen.

JCE – One of my theories is that if you make a perfume that is simple – it could be complex, but simple in how you smell it – people can add something to it, and this perfume becomes their own perfume. If the perfume is very complex, and smells very complicated, after a moment you don't want to wear it because you feel like you don't find your place in the perfume, and this sounds wrong. The wearer has to add something but you cannot say what it will be. One of my pleasures is listening to people talk about my perfume because there are plenty of stories built upon them after they have added their own mind, their own thinking, their own emotions, and this is great - not planned at all - but like evidence.

HE – In the big atrium in the lobby, when you see the big façade, you can see all the window ledges. The architect who made the building wanted it to be all glass, but as it is an atelier, people have tools and their things, so all the lower parts of the windows are a mess. Is the architect wrong? Should he have provided a closed off space where there is no glass?

JCE – It's a living effect. It's alive – you see all this mess, but the mess means life. It's very important to see that people are working, it's not a hospital. Mess is human.

HE – Some architects don't like this. They want to forbid everyone to place things on the windows. Others say, well, it's just life, you can't organize it. You can color the lower parts of the windows, to indicate that this part

of the window is out of my control. People want to be in their own place, their universe. You could see that with the workers who had pictures of their children and a few things that say this is their place and not another's. It's the same as with perfumes: architecture might be complex but it needs to feel simple in order to make everyone story's happen.

JCE – When I worked on the theme of the garden in perfume, I always took one thing, like fig which was the important thing in *Un Jardin en Méditerranée,* green mango was the important thing in *Un Jardin sur le Nil.* This way, people can understand what I want to say. If there is one thing you can grasp, you understand the story right away and you can follow it. If I put too many things you won't see what I want to say anymore, it is boring and it doesn't work. This is a rule.

HE – In architecture would you think of a building like a garden, if so, would it be a French garden? Or would it be an English garden? Maybe modern architecture is too much like a French garden - too structured, too much about getting things right. Maybe a workplace should be more like an English garden, where people can go the way they want. An English garden is not just scattered seeds; it is organized, but without being showy like in French gardens. You know that you will see that tree from the entrance. It will look like it is natural, but it is not natural. It's not a question of geometry, but more of the way you walk inside the garden, like in Chinese or Japanese gardens.

JCE – If you want to be recognized, if you want success, you have to show something important and then let people add things. You put something in evidence, and then you open it – that way people will go there and play. But the idea is not to try and say everything. Virtuosity should be perfectly organized - between the seen and unseen, the said and unsaid, in order to make the picture revealed.

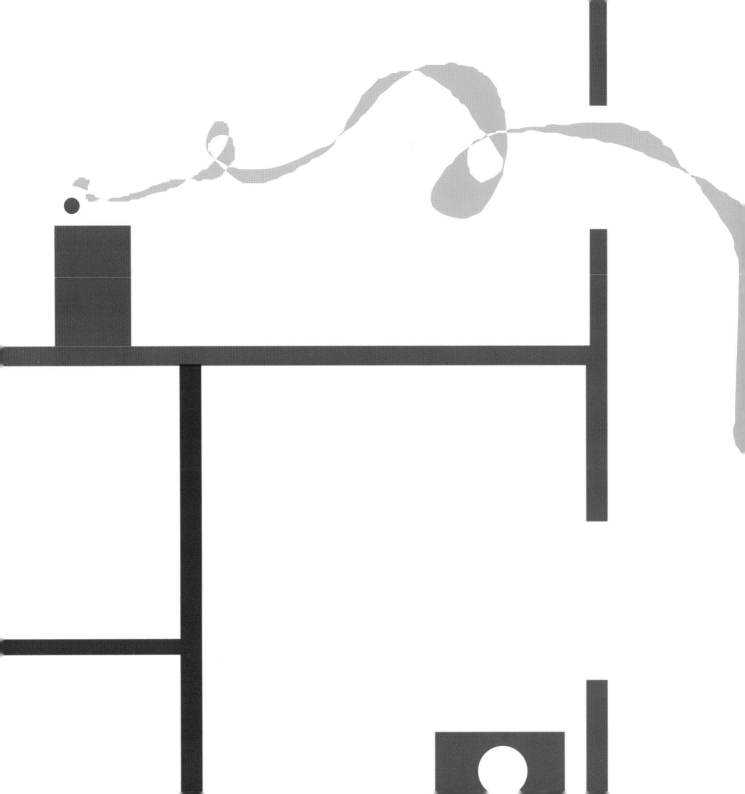

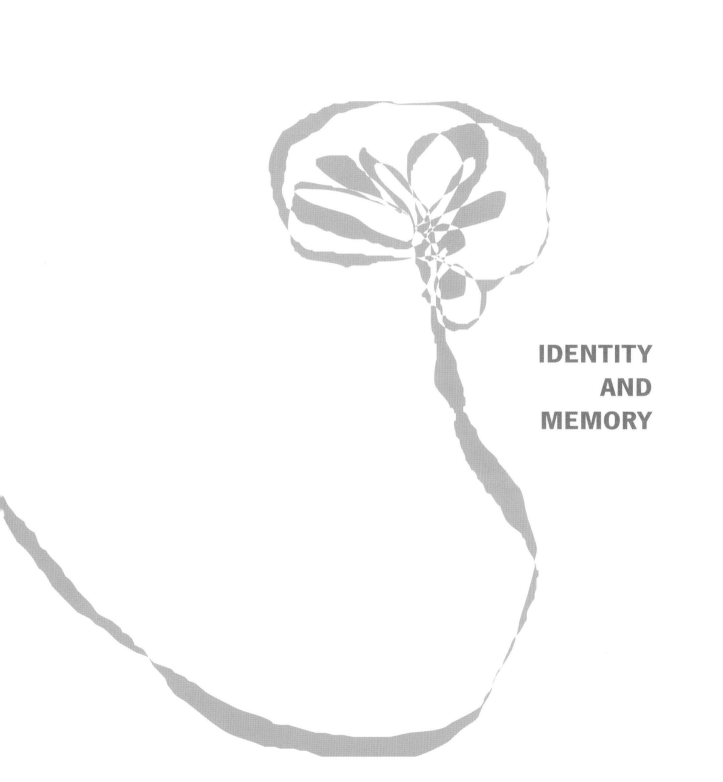

**IDENTITY
AND
MEMORY**

"To smell"

If it is true that God created light *in primis* to illuminate the cosmos, it is also true that human life is associated with dust as a molding compound infused with the breath of life. In terms of the senses, Genesis presents a sequence: sight-hearing-touch-smell-taste. We read: "And the Lord God formed man of the dust of the ground, and breathed into his nostrils the breath of life; and man became a living soul." The earthly nature of man is thus emphasized: a composition of dust, whose life is not merely animal, but imbued with the divine breath of existence, the breath of God. In Homer's Greece it was believed that thoughts and words came from the lungs and that they resided there together with words that were heard. Words were associated with respiration via a channel that connected the ears to the upper part of the mouth. While "perceive" meant "inspire" with the sense of drawing something in, the word for "look" in Aeolian meant "blow in the direction of": visual perception was not just a passive act, but also an action towards the external world. It implied an outward motion carried by the breath. That it is a question of a directed and active emission of air is better understood from the phoneme of the term for "envy" – *ftonos* – which has an onomatopoeic sound akin to a puff of wind.

Aristotle hypothesized that the senses were all connected through the organs of respiration, and thus that respiration was connected to the sentiments and that the lungs were the seat of the conscience and thought. There was a separation between mind and psyche. The former was located in the head and represented the conscience, thought, and perception, the latter was localized in the breast, being a soul understood as the breath of life which exited from the mouth (as an exhalation) at death and descended to Hades.

Today this construct connecting thoughts and the senses through breath has almost disappeared in monotheistic religions, while it is still found in peoples of animistic faiths, such as the indigenous peoples of New Guinea, who locate intelligence in the vocal organs, and in practices such as yoga and martial arts where a deeper meditation is achieved through breathing.

In English, this concept is expressed through the verb *to smell*, which is both transitive and intransitive, expressing that we both "perceive" and "produce" odors. It is an activity that has something to do with respiration, which both draws in and emits air. We are led to think of the meaning of the term "inspiration" as the initial act of Creation and of "breath" as its expression.

Non-Standard Architectures

If we were to visualize architectural forms rooted in olfactory forms what would be conjured in our minds are certainly curvilinear forms of a dynamic and non-standard nature. In *Pittura dei suoni, rumori e odori (11 agosto 1913)* [Painting of sounds, noises, and odors (August 11, 1913)] Marinetti wrote: "From the standpoint of form: there are sounds, noises, and odors that are concave or convex, triangular, ellipsoidal, oblong, conical, spherical, spiral, etc… Whereas the sounds, noises, and odors of animals are yellow and blue, those of

woman are green, light blue, and violet. We do not exaggerate if we affirm that odors alone are sufficient to create arabesques of form and color within our spirit that provide the motif and justify the need for a painting. If we close ourselves in a dark room (so that we no longer have the use of our sense of sight) with some flowers, some gasoline, or some other odiferous material, our plastic spirit will slowly but surely eliminate the sensations of memory and construct extra-special plastic wholes responding perfectly in terms of nature, weight, and movement to the odors contained in the room. These odors, via an obscure process, have become an environmental power, inciting the state of mind which for us Futurist painters constitutes a pure plastic whole."

They would be figures similar to the moving ones of Oskar Schlemmer, to the action photos of the early experiments in motion pictures, to the Möbius-strip forms and topological exercises conducted by the Ulm school. They would be the twins of the *Spatial Projections* of Antoine Pevsner. They would

107

leave prints like those of the *Useless Machines* of Bruno Munari, the mobiles of Alexandre Calder, the works of Alexandre Rodchenko, the extensions of Peter Eisenman, the variations of Bernard Tschumi…

In 2003 an exhibition was put on at the Centre Pompidou in Paris titled *Architectures non standard*. It included twelve international agencies that used numeric algorithms and calculus to create architecture that strayed from the traditional stereometric canons, and made reference to the works mentioned above as formal and conceptual matrices of this non-stereometric architecture.

The concept of the non-standard emerged from the mathematical theories of Abraham Robinson and continued through Henri Poincaré, Gottfried Leibniz, and the theory of infinitesimals that revolutionized the idea of continuum. But its relevance today makes it a candidate as the next phase to follow upon all the various post-modernist, neomodernist, critical regionalist, deconstructivist, and minimalist movements. Indeed, if these movements proposed an architecture born of a concept whose purpose *a priori* was the project and its form, non-standard architecture is produced through a controlled process whose origin and sequence are known, but whose form cannot be intuited ahead of time. Its ability to make prototypes of fluid forms and bring its instruments into the game, puts these non-standard forms into line with the concrete realization of the immaterial and of odors. These forms and their systems of management might well promise to make possible a more meaningful inclusion of odors and their expression in architecture.

Being-Essence

Paul Cézanne affirmed, in order to emphasize how intrinsic the olfactory dimension was to the experience of places, that a painting should contain within it the odor of the landscape.

The odor of a place, the odor of a building, derives from a combination of natural, iconic,

Straw Hut, Nyangatom, Ethiopia, (Fototeque Musée de l'Homme, Paris)

109

artificial, and human odors found in the space under consideration. Natural odors are associated with climate, region, orientation, pressure, relative humidity, and air temperature. Iconic odors are those deriving from the materials used, from the typical ingredients of the place. Artificial odors are due to the forced introduction of odorous elements of another nature. Human odors are associated with odors of people, but also with what is done in the place, the odor of the clothing that people wear there.

We read in a Fifteenth century alchemical treatise "[…] it is necessary to learn to recognize the fineness and coarseness of materials from their odors as well […]". In this sense the consideration of materials as "dynamic and interactive organisms", things that are able to absorb, transude, and emit, and thus modify the microclimate of a place or the quality of its air, is extremely important.

Every material has its own odor which depends on a series of factors such as humidity, porosity, temperature, and composition. The perfumer Martin Gras carried out research for years to find new woody notes. One of his resources was ENGREF Xylotheque where squares of wood arranged like books on shelves. Simply scratch the surface of one of them, even if it is one hundred years old, and its scent blooms anew.

If we look into the past we will see that each culture had a kind of abacus of odors. The Mesopotamians: cedar, myrtle, and storax. The Egyptians: incense, myrrh, juniper, benzoin, sandalwood, wine, and grapes, and kyphi. The Cretans: laurel, lavender, thyme, and rosemary. The Greeks: iris and yellow amber. The Indians: patchouli, incense, vetiver. The Native Americans: resin, sage.

In addition to the odors released by the materials themselves, odor was incorporated into oils or waxes to embellish and preserve surfaces, and also mixed into construction mortar as in the Babylonian temples and in mosques. Being is also essence, and as essence it is olfactory. For Maurice Merleau-Ponty: "The sensible is simply the medium in which there can be being, without it having to be put there", exactly as with essences in perfume. This statement brings to mind the retrospective exhibition *Scanning: The Aberrant Architecture of Diller+Scofidio* at the Whitney Museum of American Art in 2003. The two architects brought to the exhibition the walls on which celebrated works of art had been hung, with the idea that these fragments of wall were impregnated with the artistic aura of the supported work. One of them was the wall from the Museum of Modern Art on which Marcel Duchamp had exhibited his urinal *Fountain* for the first time.

Circuits and Connections

A significant issue with olfaction is the difficulty of expressing the sensations through verbal language. Speaking with experts, this lack of a vocabulary of olfactory terms is usually attributed to the tendency not to use this sense and the resulting lack of exercise in it. This is only partially true; today there are numerous systems of classification, but there is not a common vocabulary shared among the experts.

In the story about the sense of smell in Italo Calvino's *Under the Jaguar Sun*, the protagonist expresses the difficulty in describing the way his beloved smells:

"What I required of Madame Odile's specific experience was precisely this: to give a name to an olfactory sensation I could neither forget nor hold in my memory without it slowly fading."

But this is not the only reason for the lack of ability to recount odors; there are a number of evolutionary factors that need to be examined.

The olfactory apparatus is an ancient organ with relatively few direct links to the most recently developed parts of the brain, especially with the left neocortex, where our linguistic faculties are located. Instead it has well developed connections with cerebral structures that are older in evolutionary terms. These structures regulate emotion and motivation and include the limbic system, the brain stem, and the pituitary body, which regulates hormone production. The reptilian brain expresses itself via the language of instinct, the limbic system via emotions and

111

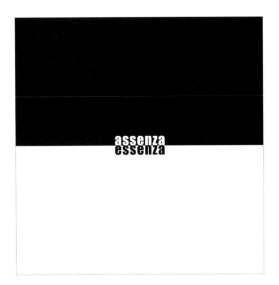

Absence-Essence by Carolina Rapetti

Absence: being absent, far away – lack: absence of air, light, gravity – a situation of uncertainty regarding the continuation of life, temporary loss of consciousness.

assenza

essenza

Essence: the set of constitutive qualities, the very nature of an entity – that which a thing is, the most important part, the fundamental nucleus of something – substance rich in aromatic elements obtained mainly from plants or flowers, used in medicine, pharmacy, and perfumery: essence of carnation, jasmine, mandarin orange.

affections, and the neocortex through words and ideas.

Olfactory sensations initially evoke emotions, which are only subsequently translated into cerebral judgments and consequently into conscious behaviors. The qualities of an odor that can be expressed through language and thus be applicable to architectural design are: class (floral, citrus, spiced, etc.), temperature, pressure, direction, and spatial distribution. In spatial terms it is important to consider the behavior of our nostrils, which do not breathe the same amount of air at the same time, but rather alternate in cycles lasting some two hours. They are connected via a cross-link system to the opposite cerebral hemisphere. The trigeminal nerve fires differently depending on the chemical nature of the stimulus, for example, carbon dioxide or menthol.

There are many different theories regarding how the sense of smell works but also much room left for exploration. These theories fall into two general categories, one based on molecules and the other on waves. The "molecular" theories are based on the "shape factor" of the molecules that stimulates a specific olfactory response and are known as the key-lock theories. This theory was proposed as far back as the first century BC by Lucretius, who believed that pungent odors were associated with atoms shaped like toothed hooks, while sweet smells were smooth and rounded. The idea is that each molecule remains in the nose until it finds a "dock" of the right form.

The "wave" theory was articulated in 1992 as a result of the research of the biochemist Luca Turin. It is based on the principle that each odor corresponds to a specific wavelength, hence to a vibration, and that the nose and the brain function as an "organic spectroscope".

Words

One of the most significant problems in the olfactory realm is notation, i.e., the system of denomination and classification for working with and talking about perfumes and other odors. There have been various and successive theories and classifications seeking to establish a common system for describing and organizing odors. However, there is still no stable vocabulary of odors that is universally shared. Each perfumery has its own.

These terminological difficulties are also related to the idea that the more terms one has at his disposal, the greater his sensitivity to odors and consequently the more developed his capacity to recognize and use them. According to Sherlock Holmes in *The Hound of the Baskervilles*, there are seventy-seven scents that an expert detective must be able to recognize. But unless we use them professionally or are passionately interested in them as a hobby, we are commonly able to recognize only a much smaller number. If we seek to determine and describe an odor, we often use terms borrowed from other sensory systems. Many words that refer to odors are concepts proper to the senses of taste (sour, sweet, rancid, bitter, strong, delicate, good, bad), touch (hot, cold, heavy, fresh), hearing (harmonious, melodious), or sight (clear, vague, dark).

In the opinion of Guy Robert, one of the major experts in perfumes, in the development of our olfactory culture we are stuck in an age equivalent to that of painters when their colors did not have names. They had to describe colors using words like "blood", "sky", or "snow". The most commonly used categories specify the following families:

"Ethereal, camphoric, musky, minty, pungent, and putrid.

"Sweet, acid, austere, greasy, acerbic, fetid (Aristotle).

"Aromatic, fragrant, ambrosia, garlicky, goaty, repulsive, and nauseous (Linnaeus's classification, 1756).

"18 categories including rose and jasmine, balsam, vanilla, camphor, citrus, eugenol, mint (Rimmel, 1800s).

"Fragrant (of flowers), putrid, ethereal (of fruit), burnt, spiced (or spicy-hot), resinous (Hennig's spatial classification, 1916).

"Floral, balsamic, fruity, empyreumatic, comestible, woody, rustic, repellent (Billot's classification, 1962).

"Ethereal, garlicky, acerbic (fruit), rancid (fats), burnt (pyretic), aromatic (spicy-hot),

The evaporating subject by Letizia Schmid

"The essence of the rose is its nonessence: its odor insofar as it evaporates." (*Glas*, *58*). Derrida's description of a rose's odor offers an understanding of identity as elusive and constantly diffusing. This *evaporating subject,* as I shall call it, not only shatters subject-object oppositions but threatens notions of fixed identities. As Derrida later explores in *Economimesis*, you are the very odor that you smell. The odor is an other, an object outside of your subjective being. But the instant you detect the odor as an odor (and can name it) is the instant that the odor and its composing chemicals are inside of you and part of your composing chemicals. *The Other Odor is not me. It is separate from me and is not I. I recognize the odor when it is inside of me, inside my nose. When its chemicals are my chemicals. The Other Odor is not, in fact, other, but me. The odor you smell is me, the odor I smell is you. You are not an other but a part of me just as I am a part of you.* When we breathe in, the space around us (the trees, the room, the car) all become a part of ourselves. The odors that surround us (and, of course, the odors that we emit ourselves) are part of our beings. Olfaction highlights the violent fragility of our identity as the space between "I" and "you/me" and "other" is subverted. There is no fixed subjectivity for the other odor is never other as it is always within me. Just as it is within you. I know that I am an "I", a distinct entity or object, when there is an other, a "you". *I am I because I am not you.* Of course, "you" does not have to be another person but any other object. Differentiation lies at the heart of naming or identification and of language itself but, arguably, there exists a part of oneself that lies outside of this process of signification. My sense of myself is more than as an object different from others. This is what psychoanalytic conceptions of subjectivity call the "split self": a "self" as a fixed object (the "I" as opposed to the "you") and the "self" that cannot be named. In an olfactory scenario, words which normally serve to establish an ontological space between two objects negate this space and conflate subject and object revealing the subject that cannot be objectified, the part of me that is more than "I". *I smell lavender* not only signifies myself as an "I" and the lavender smell as an object but also marks the instant that I am the lavender smell (and it is me) therefore blurring subject-object distinctions. Paradoxically, our identities are simultaneously confirmed and undermined, fixed subjects that are continually evaporating.

floral (fragrant), woody, musky, nauseating (H. Boelens, 1974).

That very night, first while awake and then in his sleep, he reviewed the immense ruins of his memories. He analyzed millions and millions of aromatic construction elements and classified them systematically. Quite soon he could begin erecting the first methodical olfactory structures: houses, walls, gardens, towers, cellars, rooms, secret chambers. It was an entire city constructed of the most delicious compositions of aromas. It grew larger and became more beautiful day by day, built to perfection.

Olfactory Material

The idea that a material has its own odor and that this quality can become an architectural element has long seduced many architects. Some of them have approached the odors of materials exactly as a perfumer would.

A talented designer of odorous spaces is Gaetano Pesce, an eternal experimenter with unusual dimensions in architecture and materials. His *Casa di Bahia* [Bahia House], still under construction, is oriented in that direction. It is composed of seven small pavilions made of unusual materials, for instance, rubber walls. In an interview for the catalogue of his exhibition *The Scent of Materials* in 2005 at the Milan *Triennale* he said: "I dream of walls that can wave in the sea breeze. And I would like them to give off the scent of juniper, one of the most common berries in the area."

In the *Casa di Bahia*, Gaetano Pesce experiments with three plastic materials for the "bricks": urethane, recycled rubber, and natural rubber. In order to eliminate the bad smell of the ammonia used to process the caoutchouc he added juniper syrup to the mixture, the same syrup used to treat colds. Pesce thus works a great deal with aesthetic concepts that go beyond the visual. He adds that "it is not enough for a furnishing element to be pleasant, well proportioned, or right; it has to succeed in arousing desire. It has to emanate a perfume, inspire a desire to touch it. It has to be sensorially satisfying. It has to evoke or suggest thoughts that belong to the least codifiable sphere."

In his book *Parallax*, Steven Holl, who has always approached architectural design accounting for these variables, says:

"The smell of rain-wet dirt, the texture merged with the color and the fragrance of orange rinds, and the steel-iced fusion of cold and hard: these shape the haptic realm. The essences of material, smell, texture, temperature and touch vitalize everyday experience."

Relative to these materials we must consider the changes over the past decade in the planned duration of architecture. In these buildings, which appear programmatically designed to last for less time, materials that are more experimental in nature are introduced, materials that the architecture of permanence had not yet considered. This explains the presence of certain materials like paper in the works of Shigeru Ban, curtains in the works of Petra Blaisse, etc.

Compositions

Composing with odors is a bit like writing a text.

Looking back over what we have said in this text, there are "top notes", which first seduce your nose and remain most strongly impressed in your memory for immediate recognition. We might call these "face" notes. Then there are "body notes", the second wave to emerge, which embody the structure of the perfume, the counterparts of the "bearing elements" in a building. And lastly there are the "bottom notes", which are the fixatives affecting how long the scent lasts, analogous to the "fixtures" that give quality and warmth to the work as a whole.

The different components that emerge and express themselves over the time span of a perfume have different weights and different presences, from the more volatile and evanescent top notes to the more animal and resinous bottom notes. Their purpose in the overall composition is to express the dynamic dimensions of the sensation that has to be fixed in the memory. This syntactic structure explains why literature is often associated with perfumes – or better, the literature of any given period evokes a particular perfume or array of scents since they both tend to follow the prevailing style of the period. The poetry of Baudelaire brings the atmosphere of the bordellos into the domestic setting and hence the passion for the fashion of coarse perfumes. Émile Zola associated the intellectual and aesthetic senses (sight, hearing) to the more instinctual and erotic ones (touch, smell). Huysmans gave his protagonist Des Esseintes olfactory hallucinations of red jasmine associated with the times of Louis XV. Is there a similar relationship between odor and architecture?

One of the most important noses of all time, Edmond Roudnitska, believed that the structure of a perfume was in itself a sort of architecture with its foundation, its upward development, and its crown. And as in architecture there are static, syntactic, structural, and stylistic rules. The issue of style calls to mind just how olfactory the Baroque was in its intention to compose not just forms, but sensations, movements of air and odors within its curvilinear spaces. How can we fail to think of the airy volutes and spirals joining the floors of Lorenzo Borromini's *Casa dei Filippini*

[Filippini's House]? The Baroque culture placed a central focus on the problem of perception and did not address the canons of symmetry and perfection. It explored the expressive potentials of the continuous narrative. Reading Paolo Portoghesi's writings on the Baroque regarding how the curves of Sant'Agnese and San Carlino open directly into the urban space, how their power engages the surrounding space and becomes an open fragment of a continuous oscillation, a point in which the true nature of space as mobility and becoming is revealed, we cannot help thinking of the flows of odors tracing out the same volutes and the same spaces.

Another synthesis between architecture and the sense of smell occurred during the shift from artisanship to industrial production at the dawn of the Twentieth century through the utopia of the *Gesamtkunstwerk*, the total work of art promoted by the national-regional movements Nieuwe Kunst, Liberty, Jugendstil, and Art Nouveau. Here, design was to bring together all forms of experience, including the olfactory dimension, which

119

would be incorporated into architecture in the fabrics and wallpapers that lined the interiors. Where olfactory seduction was not directly admitted, it would be evoked through formal, decorative means, as in the triumphant bronze laurels on the dome of Joseph Maria Olbrich's Vienna Secession building in 1897-1898. The "total work of art" idea entailed that everything, down to the last detail, encompassing all the senses, be part of the same aesthetic plan. Henry Van de Velde, for his own house in Uccle in 1895, even went so far as to design his wife's dressing gown.

In this panorama we should recall the works of Antonio Gaudí which achieved an extreme fluidity as had only been attempted in the Baroque. He created soft interior spaces without sharp corners or edges, fluid spaces for the circulation of air. When he was young, Gaudì had worked on the paths and grottoes that led to the holy site of Montserrat, and must have been impressed by the odor of moist earth that filled the underground spaces and moved in fluid lines, alien to right angles. Hence the forms of the Parc Güell in Barcelona built in 1900-1914. William J.R. Curtis in *Modern Architecture Since 1900* talks about the park referring to nightmarish underground grottoes, hints of shadowy clearings in some forest hidden in the bowels of the earth, and steps that flow like lava. The main terrace is supported by a hypostile hall held up by hollow cement columns, through which the drainage channels run.

Shortly afterward, Cubism was born with its fusion of abstractions and fragments of reality. It inaugurated a new relationship between spaces and ideas, between tangible materials and their invisible dimensions that proved capable of overturning the canonical forms and shaping new ones.

Vernacular, Tribal, Hypogeal

So-called vernacular architecture has a strong link to the olfactory dimension for a series of obvious reasons, one of them being that it is strongly immersed in nature and its surrounding environment, whose

Bundi Palace, Rajasthan (photo by A. Perliss, 2003)

matter it usually transforms into construction materials.

■ *Igloos* whose odor is associated with the steatite lamps that are used to heat them, to the animal skins that line their interiors, and to ice.

■ The *teepees* of the native Americans steeped in the smoke of the central fire and lined with animal skins.

■ The *yurta* of Central Asia covered with wool from the shepherd's flock.

■ The *kraal* of the Masai made of bent branches covered with dung, clay, and plant materials.

■ The Laplander *goatte* in wool, fabric, and reindeer skin with a birch-branch floor.

■ The *adobe* structures made of unburned clay and brushwood.

■ The *torchis* in northern Cameroon that are granaries in the form of enormous clay jars.

■ The walls in the dwellings in Burkina-Faso stuccoed with a mixture of dirt and oil.

■ The Dogon dwellings and Yemenite dwellings made of sand and earth, clustered together for thermal as well as structural reasons.

■ The Mexican *pueblos* and their odor of rock.

■ The *fairy chimneys* in Cappadocia with their odor of tufa.

Memory

Anyone who gets involved with olfaction will sooner or later find himself reading about Marcel Proust's celebrated pastry *madeleine* in his book *A la recherche des temps perdu* [In Search of Lost Time], where the pastry brings back to the protagonist's mind something that he had misplaced. He was just eating a piece of *madeleine* dipped in tea when he had an unexpected and extraordinary sensation. He was filled with a delicious feeling of pleasure that seemed to come out of nowhere. It made him suddenly indifferent to the vicissitudes of his life and its illusory brevity the same way love might do, filling him with a "precious essence". He felt that the essence was not in him, it was he himself. He had ceased to feel mediocre, accidental, and mortal. He had no idea where this violent joy had come from but felt that it was somehow related to the flavor of the tea and the pastry, although far exceeding it.

The sense of smell acts without forewarning; the smeller has no chance to protect himself. Olfaction does not have to enter some password to access felt emotions. Olfactory images, as opposed to visual images, do not age. They remain intact through time and resurface decades later with the same freshness as on the first day.

Human and animal memory in general is a composite thing. It has an *episodic* component and a *semantic* component. *Episodic* memory relates to the recollection of experienced events. *Semantic* memory, on the other hand, is the ability to recognize various phenomena and objects that are named through language. In the sense of smell both mnemonic processes participate, albeit in different ways. Merely smelling an odor does not necessary mean being able to name it. But when olfactory information is recorded in both registers – perceptive and linguistic – then it is indelible, as posited by the Dual Coding theory.

There is a work by Clino Trini Castelli, Frazer McKimm, and Karin Schneewind titled *Osmic Gate* designed on the basis of dual coding. It is a door and a path that stand as the entry to a Cambridge country club. It is based on the idea of contaminating a haven of the golfing elite with an odorous icon hailing from the dawn of the industrial revolution, and to do it in the country that gave birth to that icon. The pathway was crafted in Norway pine cut to the standard size of railway ties and treated with creosote. Creosote is a wood preservative that protects wood from atmospheric agents, but is also the railroad's most iconic odor from when the ties were made of wood. In *Osmic Gate* the olfactory signature had to be both respectful of tradition but also recognized as innovative.

Since odor is identity in biological terms – and also in semantic and symbolic terms – we identify, memorize, and recognize places, people, and emotional events through our sense of smell. Think of Al Pacino as a blind and depressed veteran soldier in *Scent of a Woman* when he dances the tango with Gabrielle Anwar after recognizing her smell. And then there is Robert Duvall as Lieutenant Kilgore in *Apocalypse Now* when he perceives the indelicate odor of napalm as the smell of victory, or else Andy Warhol, whose favorite smell was the lobby of the Paramount Theater on Broadway.

Mediterranean

The Mediterranean, by its inherent nature and vocation, is not a boundary separating peoples and cultures (even if for political reasons it is increasingly the case). Rather, it is a "solid sea" as the Multiplicity group defined it in 2002 at an exhibition at the *Triennale* titled "U.S.E. (Uncertain State of Europe)". The solidity of this sea is reinforced by millenary bonds, a mortar of mythology, religion, wars, trade, histories, flavors, sounds, and certainly odors as well.

In a Studio Azzurro work on the Mediterranean created in collaboration with Hermès, this concept is expressed by the wind – *anemos* – that brings life to arid land. Wind prepares and shapes the landscape, it cleans it. It scatters pollen and spores. It arranges bushes and transports trees, watering them and bringing them the heat of the south. The wind moves the waters and the sands. It carries from one coast to another the codes of a DNA that is the same all over the Mediterranean. Winds are what carry the scents of Mediterranean vegetation, the myrtle, the rosemary, the lentisk, and the jasmine so that sailors smell the land before they can see it, just as the smells of the sea are blown over the land and are all as different as the patterns that the wind forms on the surface of the waters.

That Mediterranean architectures are references to boats was certainly stated by Le Corbusier, but that the boats out on the Mediterranean are architectures is recounted by Predrag Matvejević in *Mediterranean: A Cultural Landscape*. He says that it is easy to figure out the location and type of the shipyard by the odor of the tar used on the boat, and that the construction of the simplest boats is inconceivable without the use of tar. The tar – the kind derived from plants, not the mineral tar used to make roads – is made from old pine or fir that no longer leaked sap when cut. The trunk was left to cook or smolder until all that was left was a thick, dark substance, which was then cleaned of any remaining impurities. The tar prevents the wooden planks from fermenting like wine when exposed to warmth or moisture, it protects them against rot and seals the cavities. It is also used on ropes, especially thick ones, and on barrel staves. Sometimes tallow or wax is added to it to make it easier to work with. It hardens easily and then has to be melted. It is heated over a flame and applied to the planking and between the ribs of the keel along with oakum as if it were a medicine. It makes a strong and odorous flame when it melts and leaves a dry, lightweight coal when completely burned. Tar was used as a skin ointment and also to treat gout and certain other maladies that sailors contracted in Mediterranean ports. Scents seeking to evoke the Mediterranean are as numerous as the poems, stories, movies, and songs dedicated to it. Each one aspires to capture the smell of a sea breeze, a citrus garden, or a fragment of olive-green vegetation. We will never finish adding ingredients to the Mediterranean because it is an evolving story that will not be confined. We can write nothing more poetic or complete than what has already been written about the Mediterranean, its vast and extraordinary literature that invites endless citations.

City Odors

Each place has an idiosyncratic array of odors determined by the season, the time, and its history.

In Oliver Sacks' book *The Man Who Mistook His Wife for a Hat* the author states:

"You smell people, you smell books, you smell the city, you smell the spring–maybe not consciously, but as a rich unconscious background to everything else."

It is true that cities have odors, and not in the sense of metropolitan-type smells or pollution, but in the proper sense of an olfactory essence, of an identity that at times only a few are able to recognize: there are cities that smell of curry, port cities smelling of brine mixed with rust, cities that smell musty and stale, or those pervaded by the acrid odor of burned wiring. Perhaps this is the reason why there are so

Undisclosed Recipient
by Fabrizio Gallanti

The inhabitants of Santiago have a special affection for their city. Thanks to an enviable climate and the importation of tree species from all over the world, the private gardens and public parks are invaded by multicolored flowers that bloom at regular intervals throughout the year, wreathing everything in a surprising, almost violent fragrance. There is a legend — which I was unable to verify — about a presidential decree at the beginning of the Twentieth century that ordered the planting of seeds and bulbs along the roads and railways so that the landscape would be embellished by flowers

many perfumes bearing the names of cities or places: *Paris, Un Jardin en Mediterrané, Un Jardin sur le Nil, Jaipur, Roma, 24 Faubourg…*

Grenouille, again the protagonist of Süskind's *Perfume*, finds himself at a certain point in the world's largest olfactory area: Paris.

"It was a mixture of human and animal smells, of water and stone and ashes and leather, of soap and fresh-baked bread and eggs boiled in vinegar, of noodles and smoothly polished brass, of sage and ale and tears, of grease and soggy straw and dry straw. Thousands upon thousands of odors formed an invisible gruel that filled the street ravines, only seldom evaporating above the rooftops and never from the ground below."

Paul Valéry wrote about the port-side arcaded walkways of Genoa, emphasizing their hybrid, multiethnic, Arabic flavor and their concentrated odors, the odors of frozen things, odors of spices, cheeses, and roasted coffee, and the delicious bitter aroma of finely burned cocoa. New York is associated with the smells of street vendors with their boiled hot dogs and salted pretzels. The Laurice Rahmé perfumery has developed New York-inspired scents, each evoking the specific essences of a specific part of town: *downtown, midtown,* or *uptown.*

A city that has a deep bond with water and its effluvia is Venice. Alberto Savinio wrote in *Ascolto il tuo cuore, città* [Listen to your heart, city]: "Venice is hiding this evening, but I recognize it by its odor. Odor: spirit of the mortal part of people, things, cities. Ferrara is the sister in odor of Munich. Both smell like burned stumps […] The water of Venice has its 'own' odor […] You can love Venice for its odor more than for any other reason it may have for being loved."

Open 24 Hours

The geographer Luc Gwiazdzinski, who studied the nocturnal cycles of the city, wrote that our cities have an odor that accompanies our daily and nightly activities through the different seasons. We usually forget the odor, but sometimes, with no warning, it reappears to disorient us. Evoking the odor of a city means describing a place of life characterized by ceaseless movement, by an uncontrollable and necessary closeness, where the individual attempts to obtain a personalized intimate space.

In Gwiazdzinski's book *La Ville 24 hours sur 24* there is an interview with Céline Ellena, a perfumer in the Ellena family who boasts generations of perfumers, about the iconic nature of certain odors connected to places. "La Défense has a particular olfactory fingerprint. It is a bit mineral and neutral, proper to a place dedicated to the service sector. If on the other hand, you travel through the Barbès neighborhood, a cosmopolitan place, and go into the Tati department store, your nose will certainly be surprised by the strong odors of spices and aromatic colonies coming from the African stores… That odor reassures a group of individuals who thus find some cultural continuity in space and time. Whether they are good or deteriorated, unsettling or reassuring, this neighborhood identity card represents the intimate and continuous city that stirs our emotions." But the city has its own rhythms and changes over the course of the day. Above and beyond its identity, it reflects

the activities, the seasons, and other factors that affect the nature of the odors present. In the morning Paris has the fresh smell of water along the edges of the streets, of newly applied aftershave, of croissants in the metro. But in the evening it is different.

A place almost never has the same odors during the day as it does at night because the temperature, the people, and the activities all change. Nevertheless, the cities that are open around the clock have an eternal odor that is every bit as unsettling as the rabbit's watch in *Alice in Wonderland* that always reads the same hour. They are places of constant emotion, of perennial control… from which to escape. Smells, like natural light, are the vectors resulting from a host of variables that are difficult to control completely. The 24-hour city should not fake an eternal day, but follow and respond to the rhythms and qualities of day and night's every hour.

One of the world's most famous perfumes, *L'Heure Bleue* by Guerlain, was conceived one summer evening "in 1912 when Jacques Guerlain, on his way home, stopped on a bridge over the Seine right at that moment when the sky loses the sun but no stars have yet appeared, and all the elements of nature are suffused with a blue light. It was a true homage to the Impressionists, who Guerlain dearly loved", writes Mariangela Rossi in her *Libro del Profumo* [Book of Perfume].

Linguaggio by Erminia De Luca, 2005

THE MEATPACKING DISTRICT, NEW YORK – A cobble stoned section of downtown Manhattan occupying a shrinking area sandwiched between the West Village and Chelsea. For decades, sides of beef and pork have been brought to this district to be sawed down, cut up and trimmed for distribution among the city's restaurants. Most of this industry has been relocated to New Jersey, but a few die hard establishments remain, withstanding the onslaught of fashion boutiques and restaurants.

ELIZABETH DILLER – She is a member of Diller Scofidio + Renfro, the New York based architecture firm. One of their current projects, recently highlighted in an exhibit at the New York MOMA, is designing the High Line, the park promenade that will rehabilitate part of the elevated railway that runs through the Meatpacking district.

ROGER SCHMID – He has been a figure in the fine fragrance industry for years. While working as global fine fragrance director for a major fragrance supplier he co-founded the University of the Image, a school in Milan whose curriculum focused on the five senses. His current venture is *Nose About*, multidisciplinary network dealing with scent and also its relationship to the other senses.

RS – On 9/11 I was coming back from Wisconsin, from the Johnson's Wax Building. I was stopped in Manhattan at 14th Street and I remember the smell of burning tires. All over the city: rubber. A smell that is probably now stuck in people's memory, a very powerful smell. The smell of the Meatpacking district was smell of blood.

ED – Manhattan has a particular scent – a combination of many smells. Here in the Meatpacking district the scent of blood is combined with the scent of fat. I used to live behind a sausage packing plant that exhausted near my only windows. It's a smell that I now associate with home. The post 9/11 smell lasted for some time. It was connected with the apocalyptic mood. Now you cannot disassociate that smell from death. Often bad smells are associated with badness. Good smells with goodness. Scent is tied into our morally based Christian culture. Good scent is equated with truth, honor and honesty. We over-clematize our air. We take any air bound badness out: the air: humidity, smells, heat... We want total control over the environment. It's the kind of control that neutralizes everything into nothing, a flat line condition, a culturally identified comfort zone in which everything is average - a sensory depravation. This is an economic issue as well.

RS – People have discomfort with smell, in western societies especially. Smell is a way to express something and some people feel this discomfort in expressing something through odors. There is a total discomfort with body odor, for instance. This is the antiperspirant country. The funny thing is that sometimes the smell ingredient that we put inside these products is a kind of copy of the body odor, a chemical imitation of body smell.

ED – This is an interesting perversion – control over nature again. The relation between culture and smell has been inverted in a funny way: you buy nature through chemistry, but unmediated nature is unacceptable.

RS –The smell of fast food places like Taco Bell or Pizza Hut is very awful. You even get it when you are at certain airports. This odor is terrible and invading. To me this kind of bad food is very aggressive and unpleasant.

ED – Actually I am very fond of what we culturally regard as bad smells! A bad smell experience for me is the interference of an eau de cologne with a good meal. Restaurants should have scent-free zones, like no-smoking areas. As an architect, smell is not something that I consciously design but it is in the mood set by the architecture.

ED – Air is an aesthetic medium. The Blur Building was designed as atmosphere. We engineered, monitored, and controlled it, with the expectation that breathing the building would produce a high. Blur had no walls - it was only a structural and plumbing system set on Lake Nuechâtel. We took water from the lake, filtered it and

distributed it through a high pressure fog system of 32,000 nozzles. The water is atomized into the air to make a huge cloud that you can inhabit. The water had to be very pure to be breathable as the lungs cannot deal with impurities the way the digestive system can. We were concerned about giving the Swiss public Legionnaire's Disease. We learned a lot about federal controls over air and water. If you look at any new building today, 30% of the cost is in mechanical systems that control internal climate. Generally climatization is aimed at norms, but you can see how a system can be controlled to integrate aesthetic and pragmatic desires. It is very possible that mechanical systems are the next frontier for architecture. The treatment of water, air and even electricity - we never think about it, architects are rarely involved in these fields, except defensively to protect our designs from cruel mechanical demands. Air management has to be taken away from mechanical engineers and given over to architects. We can effect atmosphere from within. When you use a perfume or a candle, you change the scent of a thing or space superficially. But designing air and scent can be thought of in an infrastructural sense. It's the difference between putting on a perfume or eating potatoes to exude an unique smell from perspiration.

RS – Again I think that it is linked with the discomfort with odors or just with education. When I enter a house and there's the smell of food, then the smell of the fireplace, the bathroom… To me this is pleasant, maybe because I grew up in Italy! You create something simply through your lifestyle without adding anything. I live between New York and Paris, and here in New Jersey I've seen the best kitchens in the world, but no one is cooking! In Paris, kitchens are as small as this table but you see wonderful food in them. Even eating too often in restaurants you miss a part of the experience; you do not enjoy it as much as you would at your home sometimes.

ED – A problem of our culture is that we are ocular centric. View is often more satisfying than the other senses put together. A lot of architects today are interested in creating special effects, whether it be acoustic, visual or atmospheric. We should pull scent apart from general atmospheres to work with it.

ED – Once I made a limited edition perfume called *No Means Yes*. I wanted to create a scent that was foul, a turn-off yet sexually appealing nevertheless. I worked with a perfumer to develop the scent and realized that I had no vocabulary to describe desired olfactory effects except by analogy. It is very difficult to express scent.

RS – In my experience developing the Helmut Lang fragrances the concept was the smell that you perceive in

the morning after being in bed with someone, after this someone has just left. We sought a very sexual, skin smell. For an exhibit in Florence, *Arte e Moda*, we had created a sperm smell reconstitution, so we proposed that! A big cultural problem is not having an appropriate vocabulary for the senses, whereas in old societies it existed. I was in British Columbia recently and they told me that among the native population still living there, the elderly people sometimes can understand who you are just by smelling you when you enter a room. They're much more linked to nature and it is impressive because it seems that we have taken away all this with technology. We thought that this was progress somehow.

ED – There's a huge technological gap in our society. We easily reproduce sound and sight the highest fidelity and high definition. But smell?

RS – Now it is possible to also do it with scent, to record, filter and reproduce a smell. This is probably where architecture could be the answer - to orchestrate the smell so that it becomes part of your wellbeing. Perhaps starting with the private home, you could discuss smell in the same way you discuss materials, colors…

ED – Since we can use, decompose, and analyze everything, how great could it be to use these technologies and scent-sensitive instruments as a souvenir collector? Military and NASA instruments applied to everyday use.

RS – Scent could be a great medium for capturing time as well – to record and select smells that might cease to exist. That would be beautiful. We should start capturing the scent of things nowadays, especially considering how things are going right now in the world.

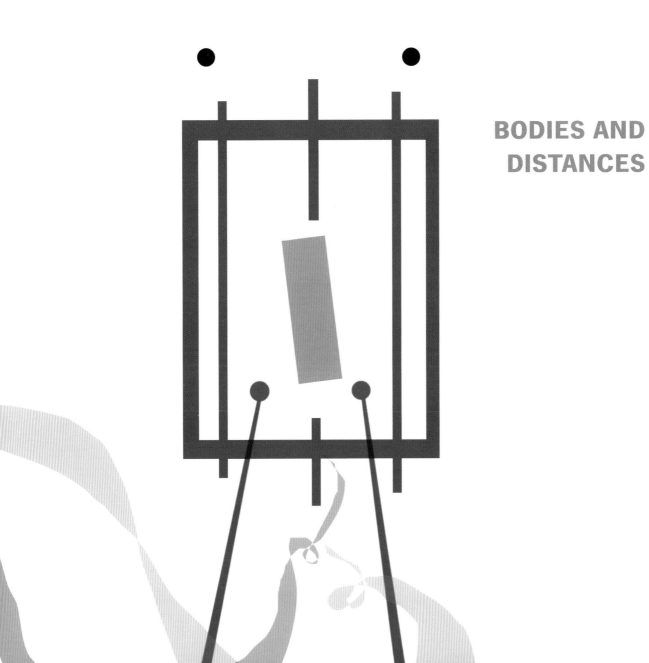

BODIES AND
DISTANCES

Territory and Belonging

Our olfactory territory is an extension of our bodies. We colonize the space around us similarly to the way other animals mark their territory.

The sense of smell is the first sense we use to explore the world. It would seem that the first sensory perception we have, before we are even born, is an odor perceived in the amniotic fluid. Actually it would seem that the spermatozoa themselves bring their own odor to the egg. When it is still functioning somewhat amphibiously the fetus can detect the mother's odor in the placenta, smelling the close presence of she who nourishes and protects, of its primary home.

This is more explicit in the animal world: the bond between parent and young is initially olfactory in nature. This odor remains in the memory as an indelible trace. We see this manifested in salmon and their spectacular migrations back to their home streams. The salmon would seem to memorize, in the embryonic stage, the odor of the pool where they were deposited as eggs. And they are guided back to it by their sense of smell, by a form of underwater olfactory orientation.

In his book *Odori* [Odors], Gianni De Martino's dwells on the spatial issue in olfaction: "Placed between the senses of distance (sight and hearing) and those of contact (touch and taste), the sense of smell has been considered a primitive, animal, instinctual, voluptuous, erotic, egoistic, impertinent, libertine, frivolous, and asocial sense, one that goes against our free will (since it forces us willy-nilly to confront unpleasant sensations) and is incapable of getting beyond the primal solipsism of subjectivity."

In this sense olfaction occupies the intermediate area of proximity, social relations, distance, proxemics, and habitation. The social history of odors is the story of our way of relating to others, their bodies, their eating habits, their rites, and their scents.

Take for example the crusade against second-hand smoking. Smokers occupy the airspace of non-smokers, they impose their olfactory space on others. Similarly, someone who wears a strong perfume invades the space of others.

Years ago in Halifax a ban was instituted against "perfume abuse" in order to prevent disturbance to others.

The situation regarding body odor is very complex because it depends on many factors, including diet. For this reason, and in spite of the fact that we live in the era of globalized consumption, our odors differ greatly from one person to the next. Between consumers of butter, animal fats, soy, and curry there is quite a variegated olfactory panorama – one that we hope endures.

The Trigeminus and the
Olfactory Compass

The olfactory organ does not have a monopoly on odors. Two other organs are also involved in the perception of odors: the trigeminal nerve (or trigeminus), and the vomero-nasal organ. Additionally, many animals are aided in determining direction and orientation by two other factors: the moist nose and the olfactory compass. A moist nose allows an animal to determine wind direction. Furthermore, since molecules readily dissolve in water, it is also more effective at capturing odors in the air. The nose is also a sort of compass. In the ethmoid bone near the nasal bridge there is a small quantity of iron. In humans it is almost negligible, but in animals such as dolphins, tuna, salmon, carrier pigeons, and bees it is found in much higher quantities and seems to play a role analogous to that of a compass needle in response to the earth's magnetic field.

In addition to factors in the horizontal plane, the olfactory apparatus is also affected by gravity. Astronauts, for example, lose their senses of taste and hearing in a weightless environment due to the nasal congestion resulting from increased pressure in the capillaries, which, like the heart, normally have to work against the force of gravity.

Furthermore, olfaction provides us with a very significant perception of height as the highest concentration of odors is found just above ground level, while odors tend to dissipate quickly higher up in the air.

In order to perceive the odor of a substance, molecules from the substance have to dissolve in an aqueous solution that our mucous membrane is able to absorb. The incessant flow of mucous is renewed every twenty minutes and works like a sort of conveyor belt, capturing odor molecules and engulfing dust, bacteria, and other particles.

The trigeminus allows us to perceive pungent odors such as ammonia. It is usually triggered at high odor concentrations, while the olfactory apparatus can be overwhelmed and practically ceases odor perception. The sensation of odor is thus in part due to the stimulation of the trigeminus. This happens in the case of ammonia when along with the acrid odor you have a prickling sensation in your nose. The fortunes of a beverage like Coca Cola have much to do with the pleasure deriving from stimulation of the trigeminus. The same is true for certain spicy foods and spiced perfumes. One characteristic of this organ is its tendency towards "dependency", where an initial aversion may eventually become a pleasure. This is the case with cocaine, tobacco smoke, pepper, mustard, curry, ginger, horseradish, and vinegar, all of which are substances that strongly stimulate the trigeminus.

According to the famous *nez* Guy Robert: "There are not good or bad noses, only people interested in odors and others who pay little attention to them. Each of us has a perfect nose. The best that I have encountered? Children between the ages of eight and twelve, whose brains are not yet sullied and do not know what they are smelling ahead of time."

Animality

In *Under the Jaguar Sun*, a book of stories dedicated to the senses, Italo Calvino defines our olfactory animal condition through the nose: "And wasn't it, after all, the same thing in the savannah, the forest, the swamp, when they were a network of smells, and we ran along, heads down, never losing contact with the ground, using hands and noses to help us find the trail? We understood whatever there was to understand through our noses rather than through our eyes: the mammoth, the porcupine, onion, drought, rain are first smells which become distinct from other smells; food, non-food; our cave, the enemy's cave; danger-everything is first perceived by the nose, everything is in the nose, the world is the nose. In our herd, our nose tells us who belongs to the herd and who doesn't; the herd's females have a smell that is the herd's smell, but each female has an odor that distinguishes her from the other females… Odor, that's what each of us has that's different from the others. The odor tells you immediately and certainly what you need to know. There are no words, there is no information more precise than what the nose receives."

Smell is the strangest of our senses as it is both animal-like and highly sophisticated. From Aristotle through to Kant olfaction was continuously downgraded aesthetically to the point where physiologists ended up considering the nose to be a simple evolutionary relic.

In the animal world olfaction can detect enemies and may even be implicated in defensive strategies, such as with the skunk. Animals that live close to the ground have a more acute sense of smell than birds, which are almost all anosmatic, except for pigeons.

There is a distinction in the animal world between microsmatic and macrosmatic animals. The latter have a well developed olfactory system and most have a moist nose allowing them to sense wind direction and thus locate the source of odors. Macrosmatics live relatively close to the ground because that is where the odors are most concentrated and because odorous substances mainly move in a horizontal direction or attached to objects.

The sense of smell is absolutely vital for most mammals. They depend on it to find food, to escape predators, and to chose mates. Sexual odors serve to attract the opposite sex and to mark territory.

There are numerous stories about animal behaviors related to the sense of smell. They all emphasize how much of our olfactory behavior is still strongly linked to our animal instincts, especially regarding sex, war, and power. For example, the panther, a scented animal, uses its scent to hunt, to "seduce" the prey, just as occurs with people, in a more veiled or more explicit way. Our sense of smell is often used in war, for example, to locate war machines or the enemy, as in the Viet Nam war.

143

Pet me

Certain animals have always lived around people. In some ways they were the original source of heating for the people and their dwellings. The presence of these animals was certainly associated with an odor that pervaded the area. However, it was probably not specifically noted but considered an integral part of a domestic landscape that had not yet been influenced by modern notions of hygiene.

Imagine the concentration of odors on Noah's Ark: all the animals in couples enclosed together in the same hold for days on end. The quest for survival and the risk of sinking probably made the odors more tolerable.

The presence of animals within our architectural structures has varied over the ages. At first they shared our space, then they were put in special stalls, then some of them – cats and dogs and some others – came back inside along with exotic animals collected on expeditions (odorous whether alive or dead). They were pushed outside again only to return as part of our dwelling spaces.

Stalls for livestock have been an element in all the most significant transformations of architecture. Think of Hugo Haring's cowshed (1925) at Gut Garkau, near Lubeck, which was a rational and modernist model of architecture for animals. The center of the shed was a fodder bin for a bull and forty-one milk cows. The hayloft was situated above this area so that hay could be directly supplied to the feed bin through a trap door. The roof sloped slightly inwards to achieve optimal ventilation: the rising warm air was conveyed towards the exterior wall, where it escaped through a continuous grill between the top of the wall and the roof. Or think of the famous San Cristóbal horse-raising farm built by Luis Barragán and Andrés Casillas in 1967 for the Egerstrom family in Los Clubes, Mexico, with the stables clustered around a pond fed by a powerful fountain of water.

Outside of domestic settings, the urban dwelling places for animals are circuses and zoos, where the animals are displayed as spectacle. Their odors are

Private Home, Miranda de Ebro, Basque Country (photo by N. Diaz, 2003)

perhaps the only remaining element of their true natures. There are some memorable structures at the London Zoo, including the Penguin Pool with its ultra-thin reinforced concrete ramps and the Gorilla House created by Berthold Lubetkin and Tecton in 1934, and Cedric Price's Aviary (1960-1963) with its aluminum frame and taut steel cables creating a lightweight and airy structure that provides maximum flying space for the birds.

Sports

Sports are performed in places filled with sweat, transpiration and the tension of competition. The odor of the gymnasium is an everyday olfactory icon relating to the oxygen uptake and gaseous exchange of active, sweating bodies.

The Maravillas College Gymnasium in Madrid designed by Alejandro de la Sota (1961) and constructed in a building with one side against the earth features an interesting play of air and sunlight on the front. Air is drawn in through a grill at the bottom of the wall, circulated in the building, and then exhausted through vents at the top of the opposite wall. The Salle Omnisports by Décosterd and Rahm is particularly interesting because it incorporates the sweat of the athletes into an overall ecosystem. Heat is produced by a convective solar heating system that heats compacted soil from the building's foundation excavations which thereby acts as a heat accumulator. The heat is then channeled into the gym and absorbed by the sweating players, who give off carbon dioxide and water vapor, which condenses on the glass walls. Plants located between the double glass walls absorb the carbon dioxide as well as the condensed water with mineral salts. By means of chlorophyll-mediated photosynthesis the plants transform the sun's energy into nutritional substances and produces the oxygen necessary for metabolizing food and providing energy to the players.

Imagine a similar system for the heavyweight "Rumble in the Jungle" between Mohammed Ali and George Foreman in Kinshasa, Zaire in 1974. Just think of the energy, the power generated! What an ecosystem!

Swimming pools, the realm of chlorine and hygiene, are also associated with odors. And it is perhaps this sense of cleanliness and health that inspired the Water Cube in Beijing which houses the pools for the 2008 Olympics and explicitly evokes the form of the water droplets gathered in the structure. The architects of the PTW National Swimming Centre assisted by Studio Ove Arup of London designed an envelope which creates the surface tension sensation typical of soap bubbles.

In auto racing we have the odor of gasoline, oil and rubber that burns the asphalt. It is a unique, pungent odor that, together with the sounds, conveys a strong sensation of the race even when the cars are hidden on the other side of the track.

Attraction and Repulsion

Odors play a fundamental role in attraction and repulsion. We are inexorably attracted by a pleasant odor even if we do not know where it comes from and repulsed by unpleasant ones even if we do not know what they are.

Civetone ($C_{17}H_{30}O$) and muscone ($C_{15}H_{28}O$) are two major ingredients in attraction and repulsion. They both derive from civet and musk, which are of animal origin, touching on the strange contradiction that we are repulsed by our own odor because we consider it to be too "animal", while we use ingredients in our perfumes precisely from that kingdom.

Among perfumes, musk is the closest to natural body odors. Natural musk is a secretion from an abdominal gland of the male musk deer, which lives in China, eastern Tibet, and Siberia. Civet derives from a secretion of the civet cat. Ambergris is formed in the intestines of sperm whales. Castor is obtained from beavers.

The mechanisms of attraction and repulsion are very complex and unraveling them is the ambition of entire industries seeking hefty slices of the market.

Oscar Wilde wrote in *The Picture of Dorian Gray*: "He […] set himself to discover their true relations, wondering what there was in frankincense that made one mystical, and in ambergris that stirred one's passions, and in violets that woke the memory of dead romances, and in musk that troubled the brain, and in champak that stained the imagination."

The relationship is certainly not so direct, not so cause-and-effect. Nevertheless, scientific and commercial experiments are carried out all over the world regarding the attractive power of odors. In London an experiment was conducted with 5-Alpha-androsterone, a human steroid secreted in the sweat and urine of males, which resembles certain components of the molecules that convey the odor of sandalwood, often considered an aphrodisiac. This steroid was sprayed on a number of unreserved seats in a theater. The researches observed that women tended unwittingly to choose to sit in the seats impregnated with that odor rather than in others that had not been treated.

Another delightful anecdote is provided by Diane Ackermann in her book *Natural History of the Senses*. She comments that many fashionable Manhattan women wear a perfume called *Pheromone* that costs thirty dollars an ounce. Drawing on scientific research into the substances animals emanate to stimulate sexual attraction, the implied promise is that it will drive the men wild with desire. But the producer did not specify which pheromone was used. Scientists have not yet identified human pheromones but they have isolated those of the boar. Ackermann was amused by the idea of a generation of young women walking about the streets of New York impregnated with pig hormones and especially tickled by the idea of what would happen if a bunch of sows were set loose there as well.

Seduction

Odor is an indispensable instrument in seduction, which is governed by the extraordinary alchemy between the likes and dislikes that draws us to certain persons and places rather than to others. There are numberless historical or legendary tales about the strategic part played by perfume in seducing a person and thereby changing the course of history. The queen of Lemnos, Caterina de' Medici, Isabella d'Este, Alexander the Great, Napoleon, and a long list of illustrious personages have had a special relationship with odors. But Cleopatra is perhaps the most distinguished of all.

Of Plutarch's many tales of the Egyptian queen, perhaps the most fascinating is how she succeeded in seducing Mark Antony by sailing to him in a barge whose sails were impregnated with rosewater: "She came sailing up the river Cydnus, in a barge with gilded stern and outspread sails of purple, while oars of silver beat time to the music of flutes and fifes and harps. She herself lay all alone under a canopy of cloth of gold, dressed as Venus in a picture, and beautiful young boys, like painted Cupids, stood on each side to fan her. Her maids were dressed like sea nymphs and graces, some steering at the rudder, some working at the ropes. The perfumes diffused themselves from the vessel to the shore, which was covered with multitudes, part following the galley up the river on either bank, part running out of the city to see the sight. The market-place was quite emptied, and Antony at last was left alone sitting upon the tribunal."

Seduction is a powerful generator of creativity and desire. It is difficult to understand why architecture refers to the body alone as a metaphor or as a formal – or even anthropo-morphic – reference, without instead capturing the more emotional and seductive dimension that bodies and places are capable of evoking. Only in rare instances has architecture been inspired by the emotional force that a body is capable of arousing, by emotional attraction, or by the seductive capacity of the inanimate.

There was no seduction in Modernism, its nudity was exposed without any coyness. Think of the transparent glass of Mies van der Rohe's Farnsworth house in Plano (1946-51), or Philip Johnson's Glass House in New Canaan (1949). The body is revealed in its entire and total nudity. Consider, on the other hand, the seductive power of Shigeru Ban's Curtain Wall House in Tokyo (1995), its corner covered by a single wind-fluttered curtain that moves to permit glimpses, to allow discovery of what is going on inside while never showing everything.

Sexuality

The sense of smell is not a panoramic sense, it is not a sense of distance; it is a tool of nearness, of intimacy and physical presence. For this reason, together with touch and taste, it is one of the erotic senses.

A body, in addition to being a receptor of odors, also emanates them. This dual direction, this reciprocity, is one of the more common activators of the rituals of sex, and of recognition and attraction. The disappearance of bodily odors, replaced by deodorizing odors, has in some way extinguished or banished certain iconic odors associated with the sites of love encounters and aroused bodies. In a 1975 article in the magazine *Casabella*, Andrea Branzi wrote that "[…] sex conditions the spatial experience, i.e., it conditions the capacity to conceive of the empty space that exists between us and others, a space that is normally understood as architectural space, as a sexual medium, as a place of free exchange of messages and relations or sexual experiences. This sort of hypothesis, sufficiently elementary to be true, is officially lacking in the history of architecture."

The places of erotic passion have always had their associated odors, initially physiological and bestial, but later characterized by increas-

ingly sophisticated ingredients for the staging of pleasure. Here Catullus is an inexhaustible source of metaphors and anecdotes that are full of olfactory references such as in the satire against Rufus to whom he writes: "Wonder not, Rufus, why none of the opposite sex wishes to place her dainty thighs beneath you, not even if you undermine her virtue with gifts of choice silk or the enticement of a pellucid gem. You are being hurt by an ugly rumor which asserts that beneath your armpits dwells a ferocious goat. This they fear, and no wonder; for it's a right rank beast that no pretty girl will go to bed with. So either get rid of this painful affront to the nostrils or cease to wonder why the ladies flee."

Over the centuries the odor of the bedroom has become increasingly sophisticated and ritualized and less natural and animal. We see this in the Casanova stories where washing the woman's body in rosewater has merely an aesthetic value; in Sade's eroticism which denies odor; or in the idiosyncrasies of

Metro Line 1, Paris (photo by A. Perliss, 2006)

Alberto Savinio with regards to a city whose foul odor he likens to "the genital reek of a detestable woman."

There are only rare cases of refined places of sex such as the *boudoirs* that the Turinese architect Carlo Mollino designed in 1938-40 for himself and his friend Devalle so they could go their with lady friends and take photos. The materials used in these interiors are glass, mirrors, aluminum, lots of curved wood, stuffing, and fabrics that unite eclecticism and personal rigor in a singularly erotic and sensual atmosphere: reflections, velvet, bodies…

Anthropology

The sense of smell has a strong social value for its capacity to foster relationships among people, and a strong anthropological value as an observatory on human behavior regarding their own odor and those of others. Tribal, animal, and social odors have the same mandate: that of identifying and recognizing members of the same tribe, corporation, or pack, and deciding who is similar and has "family" rights, and who is to be shunned.

The allowable distances between bodies are also regulated by olfactory assessments that vary from one culture to the next. For example, in European culture proximity to the odor of someone is tolerated in relation to the degree of intimacy between the source and the receptor of the odor, but the same propinquity in another culture may be easily accepted.

In 1890 Rother described the ways that the Khyoungtha hill dwellers in India greeted each other: "They have a strange way of kissing each other; instead of pressing their lips together, they apply their mouth and nose to the cheek and inhale strongly. In their language they don't say 'give me a kiss', they say 'smell me'."

Odors also condition the ergonomics and the positions bodies tend to assume in various spaces. Think of the different ways of sitting between Orientals and Occidentals, the former often sitting on the floor and the latter usually sitting on chairs. Think of how the perception of the air and the odors it carries varies depending on perceptive height. At a few dozen centimeters above the ground the oriental man has a relationship with odors that the occidental man seated with his nose one meter above the ground cannot have. The former finds himself immersed in the heavy odors that tend to move horizontally, parallel to the ground. He will smell the odor of the tatami mat, or of a carpet on which people walk barefoot. The latter will enjoy a warmer temperature and air that is neither saturated with nor devoid of olfactory elements.

George Orwell

In a well-known book by William I. Miller titled *Anatomy of Disgust* there is a reference to the sense of smell in George Orwell, not only in his texts, but also in his personal life. According to Miller, Orwell (and also Jonathan Swift) was the Twentieth century's true poet of disgust, and not the various authors such as Jean Genet and George Bataille who wrote self-indulgent pieces about pornography, sadism, and sexuality.

Orwell was incessantly tormented by ugly and malodorous things, and it was perhaps more a genuine sense of disgust than a moral sentiment. He stated that real disgust, the repugnance of unwashed bodies, bodies that intermix promiscuously, that stink, or at least smell differently from us, was the major obstacle to the success of Socialism. For Orwell, a foul odor was an insuperable barrier. If you consider the significant difference in terms of hygiene and diet between the middle class and the working class lifestyles in the early 1900s, it would be hard not to understand Orwell's difficulty in accepting a socialism based on the principles of equality across the board. He felt that racism, religious differences, differences in educational level, temperament, intellect, and even differences in moral codes could be overcome. But physical repugnance could not. He felt it was possible to feel something for a murderer or a sodomite, but not for a man who always reeked of foul breath.

Orwell's analyses were dismissed as ingenuous, but what counts is that they are based on a great truth: there are connections between olfactory emotions and cultural, racial, and social differences. Olfactory discrimination is inscribed into the story of humanity and our experience of places. Think of the institution of

153

the class system in transportation, on trains, planes, or boats. Imagine what the conditions must have been in the hold of a transatlantic liner headed for the Americas in the early 1900s.

Orwell knew well that the official odor was defined partially by that of those at the bottom of the social ladder, while at the same time it was completely independent of one's own natural odor. For this reason he was torn for his entire life between his elitist background on the one hand and his socialist leanings on the other.

Orwell's olfactory tastes conditioned his identity. He knew it was easy for him to declare that he wanted to rid himself of class distinctions yet everything he thought or did was the result of those differences. His notions were essentially *petit bourgeois* notions. In order to overcome his class orientation he felt he had to suppress both his elitism and almost all of his tastes and prejudices.

Somerset Maugham in the late Nineteenth century also reflected on the role of body odor in democracy. He described a scene in which a high ranking Chinese official sat down after dinner to speak to the most tormented of the slaves as equals, man to man, in a way that was very rare in the West. Maugham writes that the Chinese live their entire lives close to very unpleasant odors but that they do not notice them. Their nostrils are inured to odors that would drive away a European, and so they can stand with the farmer, the slave, or the craftsman. He felt that the invention of "sanitary convenience" destroyed the feeling of equality among men. It has more to do with the enmity between the classes than does the monopoly of capital in the hands of the few. It is tragic to think that the first man who flushed the toiled with a simple and negligent gesture sounded the death knell of democracy.

Fresh Air Break

During the long months spent in her hiding place in Amsterdam, Anne Frank often crouched under the window to smell the fresh air that came in through a crack.

Night Club, London (photo by N. Diaz, 1996)

155

It was a moment of ersatz freedom for the young girl.

It is quite apt that the only chance granted to prison inmates to get out of their cells and move around in a larger space, perhaps in the open air, is called a "fresh air break". In a fenced in world of limited mobility, forced proximity, and olfactory harshness, it is amusing to think of the Marquis de Sade insisting in his letters from his prison cell in the Bastille that he be sent rich perfumes. But even the prison of prisons, Alcatraz, expresses in its total isolation the paradox of air.

The island of Alcatraz, located in the middle of the San Francisco Bay, is constantly buffeted by winds and surrounded by very cold, powerful currents. Perhaps this is why it was used until the mid 1800s as a strategic military defensive position for the bay. It became a military fortress in 1860, transformed in 1907 into a military prison and became a federal penitentiary in 1934. The prison consisted of four independent cell blocks, none of which gave onto the exterior, with early underground cells for solitary confinement. The inmates had no activities except for the "mellowest" among them. The fresh air break in the high-walled courtyard and the half hour meal time were the only two moments when the prisoners were out of their cells.

Joseph Paul Cretzer, one of the prisoners, often found "The combination of smells – sharp, salty air, after dinner kitchen aromas, and perspiring bodies – once again left him slightly nauseated. No matter how many years he had spent behind bars, it was always the same day after day – that sickening, repulsive, after dinner smell". Today the only permanent inhabitants of the penitentiary are the birds and the plants. The island of Alcatraz no longer accommodates prisoners, but it is the nesting site of the West Coast's largest colony of sea gulls. Even on days when the island is crowded with tourists there are more birds than people. During the brooding season, certain areas are closed to protect the nests. A large colony of birds is also capable of producing a noteworthy odor that visitors can smell before their boat even reaches the dock.

Outside, Alcatraz island smells of guano, sea

salt, eucalyptus, and slightly sulfurous. Inside the cold prison cells one can imagine the former odors of cigarette smoke, excrement (the toilet is in the cell), and shaving lotion, mingling with the tension and fear, the solitude and boredom that must have hung in the air.

Although Alcatraz's D-Block, also known as the "Treatment Unit", had the most modern cells, they were the most feared, largely due to their orientation; directly exposed to frigid air currents whipping off the bay, these cells were used to punish problematic inmates. (One prison guard was known to use air conditioning to enhance the bitter cold.) Off in the distance the inmates could see the unreachable city, a hoped-for life, normality.

A 1999 work by Petra Blaisse was created around the fresh air break of prisoners in the Nieuwegein penitentiary in Holland. Blaisse designed a series of six gardens with crushed mussel shells, gravel, and sand giving each of them a different chromatic, tactile, auditory, and olfactory quality. An asphalt path connected the gardens to one another creating a graphic element when viewed from the cell windows.

Atmosphere is My Style

"Atmosphere is my style", wrote Joseph Mallord William Turner in a 1844 letter to John Ruskin in response to the latter's yearning for beauty in a world where it was threatened to be overwhelmed by the squalid grayness of industrial civilization.

Atmospheres is also the title of a book by Peter Zumthor, a contemporary architect who use the senses as a design tool. For him atmosphere is an experience that is more complex than architecture alone, as there can be no perception without a body, without being physically present in a place. The quality of architecture is something which is able to stir our emotions, to affect us at first glance. We perceive an atmosphere through our emotional faculties, which respond much more quickly than their rational counterpart and give meaning to our existence and our survival. An atmosphere that is coherently able to stir emotions is composed of many sensory inputs such as light, sound, temperature, and odor.

It is a total approach to architecture going beyond the purely formal into an experimental dimension that engages the entire body. This is the direction of Zumthor's works, which are masterpieces not only of architecture but also of atmosphere. Each of his buildings has its own optimal temperature, especially in olfactory terms. Zumthor and his collaborators used a great number of wooden beams in the Swiss Pavilion at the Hannover Expo in 2000. The result is that visitors inside felt the coolness of a forest on a hot day. And when it was cool outside it was warmer inside even though the pavilion was practically open-sided.

The frame of the pavilion was made of unseasoned pinaster and larch wood which was thus rich in sap and resins that released their scents into the air, giving visitors the sensation that they were in a wood-aging shed, an unforgettable atmosphere for mountain dwellers and an apt icon for Switzerland.

Istinct by Erminia De Luca, 2005

THE ZAANSE WINDMILLS, AMSTERDAM – The invention in 1596 of a crank that allowed a turning motion to be transmitted into an up and down motion, transformed this flat, windy coast into a thriving industrial center. From 1600 to 1875 thousands of windmills, churning out work in thirty-four industries, peppered the landscape. Wind generated power enabled the Dutch to saw wood (thirty-seven times faster than by hand) for boats, which, also driven by the wind, explored and colonized lands around the globe. The riches of the colonies – spices, chocolate, pigments – were then shipped to the windmills for processing.

PETRA BLAISSE – She is the founder of *Inside Outside*, a textile, landscape and exhibition design studio in Amsterdam. *Inside Outside* projects explore the boundary between interior and exterior; architecture and landscape; and the effect of movement. One of her recent large projects in conjunction with OMA was providing landscape, curtain, and carpet designs for the Seattle Central Library.

MARTIN GRAS – He is the perfumer who created such fragrance standouts as *Cerruti 1881* and *Boudoir* for Vivienne Westwood. He has conducted research on the relation of odor to music and color. He has sought unknown woody notes in European xylotechs and is involved with the fragrance possibilities of genetic engineering. Another recent project of his was reconstituting fragrances from Renaissance era formulas.

MG – In this mill there is not much odor, the chalk doesn't have much odor. We will have more odor in the paint mill, but the chalk is not giving me that much.

PB - I had a different reaction - the first smell I smelled was pipe tobacco [*from the mill operator, Piet*], very strongly, then the chalk that you can smell because of the moisture. I remember when I was at school they were still writing with chalk on the chalk board; there is this smell and the smell of the felt eraser.

MG – I did research on the pigments in Renaissance paintings for a lecture on color and odor. There is one flower whose odor is used in perfumery, and whose color is used for pigments, and that is broom, in French, *genet.* It's a bush that is full of flowers that you find all over France. That's where you have color and odor together. Broome is used in painting pigments and for dying embroidery.

PB – Dye plants and scent plants sometimes are the same. Would you describe the scent of *genet* as yellow, is there a connection? Because it works the other way around - if you see a yogurt that is pink you think it smells of strawberry, but if you put in the taste of banana, they'll still think it is strawberry. So there must be a psychological effect.

MG – You can give it a color, when you smell a raw material you want to give it a color. Now would I give the color yellow to *genet*'s odor? Probably, yes. Recently I was a judge in a rose competition and I smelled a yellow rose that had a citrus note, so there is a certain relation between color and smell. Smell has an evocative power that the other senses don't have. Only the nose can transport you directly in a situation. The nose in other times was very important, but we use it less and less. Animals have longer noses than we have. In human evolution the eyes have come out of the head and the nose is going inside, so physically we are changing.

PB – In our work we want to create atmospheres that make people happy, that put people in a certain mood. You might have perfume for the evening that lets you feel sexy if you have a meeting with a man. It has a purpose to get you in touch easier with the other sex. Other perfumes are more for during the day, to create ener-

gy or to make one fresh or trustworthy or naïve or grown up or complex… it works psychologically. And in my work it is the same - if we create curtains and materials it's not only for the eyes and the touch, but we would also want to move the air and work with scent, like in gardens. I once designed curtains with herbs sewn in the seam, so as it moved around it left this smell and nobody knew where it came from.

PB – There is something called an air curtain, a wall of air that changes the climate. This is an interesting thing - you don't see it, there's only air. In a roof-garden design we did in Korea we used a steam curtain. We created a form that you could really step into, a kind of spiral you could walk through, with two or three layers of steam. Because of the wind it constantly changes form. It would be very interesting to use in warm and cold climates and see how the difference in the ambient temperature affects the vapor drops. If a water drop gets to a certain temperature it can be like a bullet, like the archerfish that shoots a drop to catch a fly. Fantastic!

MG – Steam curtains are used in theatre too, but I am sure you can make it more interesting.

PB – Dry ice is used a lot in pop concerts. *In the Casa Da Musica* there were these clouds and it was beautiful how they would catch the light. Between the curtain, the gold-leafed walls, and the steam, there was a very nice interplay of structures and colors. But it is very important to take scent into account. There are materials, like plastic and rubber, which release gasses when they heat up and their scent comes out enormously. The projection screen that we use sometimes gets this baby doll, Barbie-like smell. Wood has a tendency to smell when it gets moist, but that has it own kind of beauty, if it's not too terrible. You realize that this scent could become an element to incorporate in a certain space. If you have wooden floors and walls, like in Swedish or Swiss architecture, you have to play with that smell.

MG – Woody notes in perfumery are very important. Trees give the perfumer more natural raw materials than flowers. When people think about perfumes they think of rose, jasmine and exotic flowers, and little about sandalwood, myrrh, *olibanum*, *ciste*, *oppoponax*, *styrax*, tolu, elemi or Peru balsam. Human beings are closer to

trees than one thinks. By photosynthesis trees transform carbon dioxide into oxygen and water into sugar, elements which keep us alive. Actually we can live on trees and will not survive without them.

There are many constraints for the perfumer in creating a fragrance. First he should have a great idea; then he is limited by the customer's price and he should be able to cope with long lastingness and diffusion. Some perfumes are long lasting but don't diffuse. Other perfumes are better at a low concentration than at a higher one. It's all a mystery! It's a lot of work to realize this great new idea; all the accords in the creation should be just right. If there is a mistake in the structure, the fragrance just "sits" on the skin and doesn't diffuse or evolve during the day. With perfume, like with music, the formula is written, but the moment of the appreciation comes and goes. A fragrance should not be three different fragrances throughout the day. It should remain a composition. There should be harmony between the top and the base. If the perfumer creates a light, transparent fragrance or a warm, dark one, the perfume should retain these characteristics all day long. The perfumer should be able to select the right raw materials and know in which proportion to use them.

PB - It's so interesting you use the same words that I do - lighter, darker…

MG – But you don't talk about long lastingness or diffusion?

PB – Well, diffusion if you talk about the effect of light and sun on curtains, because usually the curtains we make have a technical program. They have to do something to the sound, light, air or climate, or they have to create a space or change it, or shut off. But we have to think about time a lot because the moment you start using textiles, they're already degrading, they're not forever. You create things for a certain time scope and depending on the climate and the context it will survive that given time. Theatre curtains have to last 12-15 years and they have to withstand use, moving up, down, left, right, every day, for 15 years. If the climate is too dry in that building they go quicker, they fall apart at a certain point. Silk is much less long lasting; it degrades and reacts to UV light so you don't plan on using it for more than 5 years. In that sense curtains are always

very temporary, temporary architecture in a way. This is ok, because as the culture, the client, the organization or whatever, develops, in ten years they might have a different mentality anyway, so they would like to change the color or the symbol of the building. With gardens you have the opposite time scope. Gardens need a lot of time. You plant them and then it takes 5-10-15 years before they look like anything that you imagined. If it's not hard material, if it's planting, with soil and grass, you need conditions that help it grow and survive.
PB – People leave their traces on a building. So does the landscape, the context - these make the building what it is in the end. The smells of an identical building in Seattle or in Ho-Chi-Min City are as different as their respective temperatures and climates. The climate created by the inhabitants and the natural climate - airborne salt and micro-life - have an immense effect on the life of a building.

MG – Home designers should start from interior design before going to exterior design. We had one fragrance project inspired by the Mexican architect Barragan, which became something very interesting. With fragrance you can build a theme. If you have a room which is very warm or very cold or clean or Japanese you can build that into your fragrance.

PB – But how? Psychologically?

MG – No, by the way you feel, the way you feel the place is. Physically you don't see it, but it is the way you feel in it.

PB – But you're saying that you can implement it in your perfume you're making? The ideal Japanese space?

MG – Yes, but it still will have to be a perfume – this is what the problem is. Clients demand creative things from perfumers, but its like the rose competitions, you have to pick the best smelling rose, which must smell like a rose, otherwise it is out of the picture. It's the same with fragrance: when you make a fragrance, it has to be a perfume that you can wear. So the frame should be there, and inside that frame you can create whatever you want, what you feel, and what the client wants you to do. But it's got to stay a perfume, and not only

an odor. PB – In what I do there is a problem which is "lifestyle", the syndrome of putting scent in the living space, which I have an allergy against; like in the taxi where you get this horrible synthetic pine tree deodorant, that debilitates your brain. I am not thinking in that mindset with my work, at all. I used to design exhibitions and in one project for OMA sound was supposed to influence your sense of space. In a very small room, totally dark, there were models of city planning. Then we had sound that made you think that you were in an enormous echoing space, like a tennis game where the ball goes *tock… tock*, or a train passing endlessly. We used these sounds to emphasize what the architecture was about, and also for the viewer to emotionally understand architectural scale. In that sense we did it in a synthetic way but it had an amazing effect. With textile you cannot create sound, (except that you can hear and feel it when a cloth or a curtain moves through the air), you can only filter it or reflect it, or absorb it. Did you ever use the scent of grass? It's a very spacious scent.

MG – It is the outdoors, so automatically you smell it and you feel outside. It can be imitated with only with only two synthetic raw materials, *cis 3 hexenol* and *cis 3 hexenil acetate*. Many years ago we analyzed the odor of grass and found over 50 raw materials or molecules.

PB – So you imitate it with synthetic molecules, you don't use real grass?

MG – We can imitate a flower almost 100% and we can even make it smell better. That's why we don't do any extractions or distillations out of the lily of the valley or carnation. Most of the synthetics we use are analyzed in natural oils and synthesized, so they are not synthetic-synthetic. They do exist in nature and with synthetic molecules we can emphasize certain characteristics of flowers; we can improve upon them, for instance, by pushing the spicy note in a carnation or the fruity note in a rose. When a customer imposes an extremely low price, the perfume risks to be too synthetic and smell "cheap". A fragrance needs to have a certain percentage of natural oil, to give them richness and beauty. You can't cheat on quality and the best cooks agree.

PB – It is weird that with perfume there are the same tendencies as everywhere else. It's so parallel to social shifts, or economic shifts, but surely not political shifts; do you have different perfumes now that we've got rightwing Christian governments?! Bush, Berlusconi, Balkenende…?

DRY AND HUMID

Epidemics

Prior to Louis Pasteur's discoveries in the mid Nineteenth century it was believed that the air was a vehicle for disease and that odors were a manifestation of the air's filthiness. The history of the foundation of cities, their orientation, and their urban plan, can be considered in relation to epidemics. Vitruvius captured this concept in his treatise *De Architectura*, where he advised against building a city near a swamp because "[…] the breath of the monsters living there can infect the place".

The Greek and Roman cities were absolutely impeccable in terms of the urban quality that was achievable at those times. It was with the Medieval cities that the first complications in terms of population density and air quality emerged. During the Middle Ages it was thought that diseases such as the plague entered the body with the breath. Hence treating the air, perhaps simply by sweetening it, was thought to be a means for combating this pestilence. Sweet scents were considered an antidote and so the early onset of an epidemic was fought with bonfires of pine, fir and other scented wood set alight in the streets, one bonfire kept ablaze day and night for every eight houses. Sulfur was thrown onto the fire periodically, producing dense and acrid fumes that caused lachrymation, rhinorrhea, and a burning sensation in the throat. The doctors who were forced to visit and treat the sick were completely covered in protective clothing. They wore long leather overcoats coated on the inside with honey-scented beeswax, thick protective gloves and peculiar beak shaped masks that were filled with fresh herbs and dried flowers.

During the Black Death in fourteenth and Fifteenth century Europe, enormous quantities of perfume, aromatic herbs, and potpourris were used in the attempt to rid the air of the pestilence and keep it far from the body. Resins and gums were also burned in the torches to perfume the air. Around the homes of the sick or dead a huge quantity of "plague water" containing aromatic substances was sprayed in order to create a sort of sanitary and olfactory cordon. Eau de Cologne actually originated as "plague water".

During the great plague of Marseilles in 1720 three fumigations were done: the first with aromatic herbs, the second with gunpowder, and the third with arsenic and spices. It was not until 1788, with the discovery of Javelle Water, or bleach, that the idea of disinfecting with perfumes was supplanted by chemistry.

Erasmus and the Birth of Manners

If the history of odors is linked with the evolution of personal and social manners, a fundamental moment came in the Sixteenth century with the first publication of *De civilitate morum puerilium* by Erasmus of Rotterdam.

Erasmus's treatise had a strong influence all over Europe because it was a work addressed a broad audience with no class distinctions. It was a sort of manual that went beyond culture and custom, presenting universal rules to help people emancipate themselves from their miserable conditions. Children were focused upon; as the link between the emotional animal and the rational adult, their upbringing and education were very important.

Erasmus was thus the forebear of a new standard of chastity and aversion, although hygiene was not a frequent issue in his work. His directives aimed at liberating natural functions instead of repressing them, which he felt could lead to disease. It was only later, especially in the Nineteenth century, that these indications would be interpreted as prescriptive tools serving to enforce self-restraint and a repression of instinct.

His treatise thus had a significant impact on childrearing and consequently on future generations. His educational approach aimed to make desirable social behavior an automatic thing, making it seem to each individual that a given desirable behavior arose from his or her own autonomous initiative, from an innate desire to ensure human dignity. These principles would become dominant with the rise of the middle classes. Erasmus's book was grounded on the concept that the exterior manifestations of the body were an expression of the inner reality.

In his book *Power and Civility. The Civilizing Process*, Norbert Elias included some excerpts from Erasmus regarding bodily emissions and their propriety. These included the statement that repressing natural flatulence is an act of idiots who attribute more value to civility than to health. In his *Diversoria,* Erasmus addressed the differences between the customs in French and German inns. He described the dining room in a German inn as follows: "Some eighty or ninety people are sitting together, and it is stressed that they are not only common people but also rich men and nobles, men, women, and children, all mixed together... One washes his clothes and hangs the soaking articles on the stove. Another washes his hands. But the bowl is so dirty, says one speaker, that one needs a second one to cleanse oneself of the water. Garlic smells and other bad odors rise. People spit everywhere. Someone is cleaning his boots on the table. Then the meal is brought in. Everyone dips his bread into the general dish, bites the bread, and dips it in again. The place is dirty, the wine bad... The room is overheated; everyone is sweating and steaming and wiping himself. There are doubtless many among them who have some hidden disease."

Morality

In the Third century BC Diogenes warned: "Beware lest the sweet scent on your head cause an ill odor in your life." The moral conviction that Good smells nice and Evil stinks has roots that reach farther back than Nineteenth-century bourgeois morality.

In the thirteenth and fourteenth centuries the plague forced the closure of the major European bath houses leaving people with no alternative but to wear perfumes in place of daily bathing, as had already occurred for the ancient Egyptians and Mycenaeans. In the Middle Ages plants were used as a means of protection, while perfumes became vehicles for the pleasures of the flesh. Almost no one washed themselves or their clothes.

The Council of Trent (1545-1563) forbade public baths in the name of morality. But this had no influence on the private dimension of cleanliness. Personal cleanliness began to be valued and the consumption of personal cleansing products increased.

In the Eighteenth century the French courts were clean only in appearance. Everything was whitened with a cosmetic powder that was applied everywhere, even on people's wigs. The expense for this item at the court of Versailles was enormous, much more than the cost for food, and such expenditures by Josephine de Beauharnais provided delightful fodder for the chroniclers of the local *gazette*. It was only when people began to believe that it was all a question of bacteria and microbes instead of the machinations of the Devil that civilization surged ahead. The Paris of Haussmann incarnated the idea of both hygienic and moral purification. It was no coincidence that the plan entailed reorganization of both the "upper" and the "lower" city.

Utopias and Hygiene

February 14, 1790 was a critical date in the history of hygiene. Jean Noel Hallé, who four years later would become the first public health director of the newly instituted Paris bureau, made the first olfactory survey of the Seine riverbanks to assess its environmental quality. This investigation would soon usher in a public debate on the disposal of excrement, sewage, and waste in France and all over Europe. Many grand and even utopian projects would grow out of this.

The real fear, on the part of both hygienists and utopians, were epidemics, which were thought to be caused by the stench that reigned everywhere. In many countries the hygienists succeeded in combating the strong malodor of cities, hospitals, prisons, and dwellings with grandiose projects. They built covered sewer networks, installed ventilators and bellows, closed factories, equipped hospitals with "commodes" that had extractible pans, treated cemeteries with salt, lime, and hydrochloric acid, drained cesspools, established regulations for sewer-workers, drained fetid swamps, patched, stuccoed, and painted walls, ceilings, and roof beams to protect against the external miasmas, and even applied "antimephitic" paints to furniture.

The first municipal public health units were also established.

One of the more common issues was the deodorizing of crowded public places. This involved controlling and managing air circulation to guarantee an adequate supply of fresh air to all spaces. A new season of studies on ventilation was inaugurated thanks to Tredgold in Britain, and to D'Arcet and Peclet in France. Their research focused on a hermetic room for treating persons with pulmonary tuberculosis so that they would not have to spend long periods far from home. One room was transformed into a climate-controlled greenhouse where the chimneys were closed, the windows sealed, and the doors were prevented from fully opening. In 1821, Arcet's doctor created designs for a stove with sufficient aspiration so that no ventilation via doors or windows was required. The use of wind and machines, especially bellows and forced air ventilation systems flowing towards a heat source, found wide practical application. However, in the French capital the latrine ventilator – to evacuate odors – was the only device in widespread use.

In 1844 Tony Garnier dreamed of building a vast industrial complex for treating urine with the proposed name "ammoniapolis".

As the industrial revolution changed the odor of cities and architecture, the moral value of perfume reached a peak. Those who were morally fit were also nicely scented, and vice versa, those who stank were closer to beasts on the social ladder. We still carry the prejudice that those who are in constant contact with bad odors are at the bottom of the professional scale: sewer workers, bathroom cleaners, "sanitary engineers", agricultural workers.

The Bourgeois Home

Whereas the separation between public and private space on the urban scale became an unavoidable issue following the French Revolution, it was estab-

Steam House by Steven Holl at Cranbook Institute of Science, Michigan (photo by S. Holl, 2004)

174

lished more slowly inside the home, in the wake of changes in the role of children, women, hygiene, customs, and morality that had begun in previous centuries.

Leaving behind the heterogeneity of the Middle Ages and the "shotgun" arrangement of interior spaces in European courts, the Nineteenth-century house was a labyrinth of sensorial deprivation and seclusion: visual, to screen oneself from indiscrete eyes outside of the family nucleus; auditory, to contain the voices of solitude described in secret diaries; and olfactory, as a hypocritical epiphany of a perfect world.

Heterogeneity was combated both on the functional and the olfactory level: there was a scent for every room, and they were never allowed to mix. The abolition of olfactory mixes separated the areas for preparing food from those for eating it, it barred the doors of the bath and the toilet, it separated organic odors from decorative scents. These latter were then employed to create a new olfactory aesthetic within private spaces.

The house was still insufficiently illuminated and overadorned with fabrics that made it a sponge for odors. In spite of the fact that the use of corridors, stairways, and passageways now allowed independent access to each of the rooms, the air circulation was still insufficient to fully aerate the interiors. Odors thus found niches where they would stay and endure. At the end of the century the bourgeois dwelling still smelled of residual and stagnant odors that did not reconcile well with the social intentions of cleanliness and hygiene.

The rooms adhered to an olfactory protocol that illustrated many of the qualities of those who lived there. At the beginning of the Twentieth century the internal arrangement of the middle class dwelling was still patterned on the moral laws of the previous century: a house with dark hallways and rooms enclosed within other rooms behind closed doors.

The unchallenged ruler of the house was the woman, who became the warden of the private realm, but also its prisoner. Here odors became the yardstick of chastity and morality.

The use of makeup on the part of morally irreprehensible ladies was reduced. Analogously in the household environment the balance between produced and applied odors followed the same rule of sobriety. Applying scents to spaces and to oneself became a question of hygiene and not the manifestation of a desire to seduce. The representation of morality became more important than morality itself and its physiognomy redesigned the domestic space.

The bourgeois house is still an enduring model for many with its curtains and slip covers chastely hiding forms, with room deodorizers, air conditioning systems, and ready-made theories of order and cleanliness.

The Dry Century

During the Twentieth century the idea that cleaning did not simply mean washing, but substantially draining, introducing oxygen via movement, became incontestable. The great enemy was stagnancy, accumulations resulting from situations where more was produced than could be assimilated.

The Twentieth century was when spaces became dried out via sunlight, dehumidification, and the use of hard and impermeable materials. And it was precisely these methods for drying, dehydrating, and waterproofing, along with the use of non-breathable materials that pushed odors into oblivion and disaccustomed people to the presence of odors in architecture. The study and creation of scents was relegated to perfumeries and applied arts and all that remained outside of the refined toiletry bottles was labeled as malodor and banished.

"Light and air for all" was the motto of the campaign against tuberculosis trumpeted by the architects at the International Congress of Modern Architecture (CIAM). The popular housing projects of those years, from single family dwellings to medium and high density dwellings, were aimed at improving the hygienic conditions of the residents, natural lighting conditions, spatial orientation, and air quality. The logical outcome was the abandonment of closed blocks in favor of row houses, the only housing type that provided the possibility of good orientation to all the lodging units.

Modernism designed interior air quality for functional and not poetic reasons. The odor of architecture was not an explicit design component, except perhaps in rare cases, but it was nevertheless present and perceived in works of that period. At times it reinforced the concept behind the work, other times it shifted the perceptive focus away from the functional center of mass to create surprising, interesting, or misleading aesthetic interpretations.

We always wonder how much the insistent smell of thyme in certain works of Alvar Aalto or Gunnar Asplund was tolerated or desired, how much Mediterranean odor reached the rooftop gardens of Le Corbusier, how much odor of agave and scorched desert insinuated itself into the houses of Richard Neutra in Palm Springs, and what blend of tires, asphalt, and mountain breezes was breathed on the rooftop track at Lingotto in Turin, built by the engineer Giacomo Mattè-Trucco to test drive the early FIATs. What is certain is that the odor of a place is always there, even if we would like to abolish it. Actually, eliminating it becomes such a daunting design task that it is often ignored in the hope that it will not interfere with the result.

In its material dryness and dehydration, Modernism achieved an ideal that was at times aseptic, a clinical and medical aesthetic devoid of emotion and corporality. But in a place without odor the body is lost, it loses one of its fundamental compasses and is left feeling vulnerable. The urgency of smelling the odor of the air becomes not only a means for judging its quality, but also a way of determining the setting in which one finds oneself. Perhaps it is for this reason that contemporary architecture now seeks humid materials with an olfactory memory. It is introducing gels, which are simply colloidal suspensions of macromolecules in water, pulps, "non-woven textiles", or felts that are nothing other than wool or other processed materials.

Vapors and Fog

In order for an odor to be perceived it has to

dissolve in an aqueous solution to that the mucous membrane in the nose can absorb it. Water as an olfactory solvent provides the essence of certain iconic places related to odors: brine, the flowing water of the fountain, stagnant water in swamps, sulfurous spa water… eau de cologne.

We are beginning to see a significant number of contemporary projects that dedicate attention to the humidity of the air and even emphasize its presence in the form of vapor or fog, to underline our emancipation from the idea that humidity is a vehicle for filth and a synonym for unhealthiness.

One of the early works created in this regard was Shoei Yoh's *Prospecta* (1992) in Japan. It was a hollow cube conceived as an observatory on the surrounding landscape. The surrounding nature was the object of observation and the natural spectacle was enhanced by special effects produced by a machine that released smoke, light, and musical effects.

In *The Mediated Motion* installed in 2001 at the Bregenz Kunsthaus, designed by Peter Zumthor, the artist Olafur Eliasson superim-posed over Zumthor's rigorously orthogonal cement and glass architecture an invisible architecture of perfumes, fog, water, plants, and soil.

The architect Ned Kahn creates works that aim to show the expressive dimension of vapor, clouds, and air vortices, as in *Infalling Cloud* (2000) at the Rose Center for Earth and Space in New York. His *Cloud Rings* (1993) at the Exploratorium of San Francisco was a prototype for the Providence, Rhode Island airport terminal, where the architect sought to create the sensation of flying among the clouds. Another work, *Invisible Whirlwinds* (1987), at New Langton Arts of San Francisco produced a slender tornado using fans, curved walls, and the gallery's ventilation system. Movements in the gallery altered the air currents and changed the form of the vortex.

A notable work by Steven Holl, one of the architects on the international scene most attentive to sensory and perceptive issues, is the Steam House at the Cranbrook Institute of Science. The building is a sort of experi-

ment in living in a very humid environment, with all one's biological water requirements provided not through drinking, but through skin absorption. By means of a special nozzle, each drop of water is atomized and pressurized until it is so well airborne that it does not condense on the walls or on visitor's clothes.

But the work that marked the threshold between material and immaterial architecture in architectural imagery was *Blur Bar* by Diller and Scofidio at the Geneva Expo in 2002. It was a sort of lightweight pile dwelling structure made of a delicate network of water pipes standing over a lake. The structure was outfitted with a system that extracted water from the lake and nebulized it to completely saturate the surrounding air, creating an artificial cloud that changed shape and consistency with changes in wind, temperature, and humidity. In this "building", Diller and Scofidio expressed the possibility of eliminating all traditional architectural elements down to the structure, constituting an architecture of sensations, of impalpable yet immanent elements, which are ethereal in the same manner as a perfume.

Spas, Baths, and Saunas

The civilizations prior to the Romans certainly had running water in their buildings: *terracotta* pipes brought water into the baths and ran water under the lavatories of the Palace of Knossos in 2000 BC. The Romans, however, unlike the others, designed drainage systems for entire cities. There were faucets in the houses for running water; hot water ran through pipes from the boilers atop the furnaces to fill the baths; and there were individual lavatories. Heating largely took the form of coal carried from room to room, but in cold lands such as Britannia and Gaul and for country villas and public baths the *hypocaustum* was used. This was a raised brick floor heated from below by furnaces. Hadrian's Villa, built by the emperor in the First century BC, was an eloquent example. The

Thermal Baths by Peter Zumthor, Vals, Switzerland (photo by A. Barbara, 2005)

emperor wanted to incorporate into his villa all the buildings that had impressed him during his long journeys. He also had a spa put in, comprised of two complexes, the Small and Great Thermal Baths, whose rooms were always kept warm by an elaborate heating system.

Of equal fame are the Baths of Caracalla in Rome encircled by gardens and gymnasiums. They had a circular room with a domed ceiling that was divided into a warm room (*tepidarium*) under the roof, and an open-air room with a swimming pool (*frigidarium*). The bathing process began in the *unctuarium* where the people selected ointments and scented oils for their massages and the very humid air was thus always strongly scented.

In the Arab culture, the *hamam* have always been scented places. Julia Pardoe, a Nineteenth-century English traveler, described the *hamam* in Istanbul as a phantasmagoric scene filled with heavy, dense, almost suffocating sulfurous vapors. Bathers were soaped up at the entrance, then scrubbed, rinsed, and perfumed. After the bath the bathers relaxed around the sides of the pool under the dome where they ate sorbets and serenely smoked the long pipes known as *chibuk* among the sulfurous vapors.

Turkish baths, saunas, and spas have always been associated with an idea of cleanliness and salubrity, and here odors play an important, balsamic role. The thermal baths designed in Vals in 1990-96 by Peter Zumthor are perhaps the work of contemporary architecture that most strongly picks up the idea of spa architecture, translating it (a decade before everyone else) into an extraordinary project. The building breaks with the tradition of baths from the 1920s, which focused on the principle of light and air everywhere. One side of the Vals Baths rests against a mountainside, and the others are open to a mountain range, offering beautiful panoramas from every window and opening. The interior, faced in local gray stone, is immersed in water at various temperatures, and each bath releases its own bouquet of vapors. Your body becomes one with the water which seems to flow through and purify it. The small rooms with the various baths all have a sensory emphasis: temperature (hot or frigid); auditory (reverberation tank); or olfactory (the rose pool).

Natural and Forced Ventilation: the Beginnings

One of the central themes in all of Twentieth-century architecture was how to ventilate a building, and architects came up with various methods for accomplishing it. There were two basic and opposing approaches: on the one hand there were those who sought to take the air from outside and to bring it into the building without changing its olfactory qualities, only modifying it in terms of temperature and pressure. The other approach, a bit phobic, was to cut off all relations with the exterior air via extreme filtration and forced flow, using technologically complex systems such as air conditioners.

If we look at three masters of modern architecture we find three very diverse attitudes and approaches.

Of the three, Frank Lloyd Wright was the one who most strongly contemplated the air of the setting into which his work would be incorporated and included it as a design element. Most of Wright's houses were built in extremely meaningful natural settings, such as Oak Park, where he built the first prairie houses, or Bear Run, where he built the celebrated Falling Water house for Edgar Kaufmann in 1935-39, or else the Barnsdall House of 1917 on the outskirts of Los Angeles where the city meets the desert and there are olive and citrus groves that exist thanks to irrigation.

The air circulation inside these houses was the fruit of meticulous design for their heating and cooling. But the air was also humidified via water flowing in and out of the houses through openings in the walls just below the roof, making them "breathe"

Le Corbusier's relationship with air was quite controversial. He developed solutions to support natural ventilation, such as the *pilotis* in Villa Savoye, the openings in the roof of the Beistegui House that transform the highest rooms into air chambers, or else the aeration chimney on the roof of the *Unité d'Habitation*.

183

But when he turned to the use of machines for forced air ventilation the results were catastrophic. In 1929 Le Corbusier and Pierre Jeanneret were engaged to design the *Cité de Refuge of the Salvation Army* in Paris and built a building with a façade in hermetically sealed glass for the dormitories, designed to house 900 refugees. There ended up being 1,500. While winter passed under pleasantly tepid conditions for the guests, the same rooms in the summer were transformed into such ovens that Le Corbusier had to modify his designs to allow the windows to be opened and install partial *brise-soleil* to avoid being sued by the City of Paris.

It was Mies van der Rohe in his Lafayette Park apartments in Detroit who integrated a forced air ventilation system perfectly into a specially designed frame located under the windows. The tenant thus had the choice between controlled natural ventilation and the option of installing an air conditioner.

The Wind Rose

Architecture for the sense of smell is like a large ship that responds to the winds, which opens its sails to the southwest wind differently than it does to the north wind, which steers by the sun and furls its sails when darkness falls.

Vitruvius writes about urban design in *De Architectura* stating that after the outer walls have been built, the distribution of the lands within the walls had to be worked out as well as the direction of the streets and alleys according to the behavior of the sky. The orientation of the streets was important to prevent them from becoming wind tunnels. The offending cold winds, the vitiating hot winds, and the moldering humid winds had to be excluded by orienting the streets perpendicular to them.

The same thoughts are found in an interview by Hans Ulrich Obrist with Cedric Price, who told about participating in a design contest for an area on Manhattan's West side, considered the island's last open area. Price wanted to avoid placing obstacles in the way of the wind, to avoid creating areas of stagnant air. He designed a building where the air could enter through windows, doorways, and curtains.

In oriental architecture the curtain shows how air blows through the building, showing its direction and the scents it carries. Here it is clear that the value of the curtain in contemporary architecture cannot be ignored, especially not when it has such an extraordinary interpreter and experimenter as Petra Blaisse. The curtains created by Blaisse and the studio she directs, Inside Outside, are based on the concept that the curtain is not a barrier, but a second "smart" skin for the building, a membrane that screens the wind, sun, sight, hearing, touch, and certainly the air. It was a striking experience for many at the *Movements* exhibition in New York in 2000 to find themselves confronted by a huge building-sized curtain mounted externally rather than internally. It was a spectacular operation, a cross between Land Art and advertising, between macrodesign and architecture. That it was something more than a curtain was immediately clear, and a few years later Blaisse took part in the *Skin* exhibition at the Cooper Hewitt Museum, with an unequivocal explanation of her works: they are not curtains but skins, soft and breathing skins for the architecture of a new-dawning millennium. The skin designed by Blaisse is inscribed in the identity of the building, but it can also be a landscape with coy vegetal macrographics as at the Illinois Institute of Technology in a work by O.M.A., or at the Danish Embassy in Berlin in 2000. But they also function as acoustic curtains and theater curtains as in Grand Palais in Lille in 1994, and the Second Stage Theater in 1998.

In the works of Ned Kahn the wind becomes a sculptor of the façade. His Technorama Façade for the Swiss Science Center in Winterthur (2002) is a wall composed of thousands of aluminum panels that move with the air currents and render visible complex turbulence patterns. A similar effect was achieved in the *Wind Veil* at Gateway Village, North Carolina in 2000, where the façade of a new parking structure was covered with 80,000 small aluminum panels fastened in such a way so they could move freely in the wind. From the outside, the entire wall seems to move with the wind. Another project, *Slice of Wind*, at the College of Engineering at the University of Colorado at Boulder in 1996, used 10,000 disks installed above the main entrance to the building that responded to the wind to create digital images which changed with the passage of air currents.

History
by Erminia
De Luca, 2006

GIARDINO DEI SEMPLICI, FLORENCE – The world's third oldest botanical garden, established in 1545 in response to Cosimo de' Medici's desire for a garden of medicinal plants. Over time it grew in value to become a cultural institution. Today it occupies an area of 23,892 square meters with greenhouses of noteworthy size in terms of both area and volume. Some greenhouses keep a relatively warm habitat for tropical plants, while others are cooler for plants from more temperate climates. The medicinal plants grow outside. Of particular note is a European yew planted in 1720 and a huge oak from 1805.

CLINO TRINI CASTELLI. Design professional and theoretician, he was the first to concentrate on the emotional value of products in industrial applications. He has received two Compassi d'Oro and the IBD Gold Award. He is among the pioneers in design and architecture to explore the points of convergence between design and odors.

LORENZO VILLORESI is a perfumer known the world over for his prestigious olfactory compositions for Santa Maria Novella in Florence, the world's oldest pharmacy. His interest in perfumes is nourished by an extraordinarily varied range of cultural interests, including ancient history or philosophy. He traveled extensively through Northern Africa and the Middle East before embarking on his professional career.

LV: The spatial design of a perfume interests me well beyond the creation of products. Right now we are designing a top for children with the intention of creating a sort of "olfactotheque". The idea is to provide children with the opportunity to get better acquainted with and interact more with the universe of fragrances, both with smells they already know and with those they do not. So we decided to built a truncated cone with icons and images of plants all around its circumference. The alternative would have been one with a geographical theme, but this would have had the same limit as the manuals; it would only have been able to accommodate a small part of the materials actually used. Natural fragrances are only a small part of the world of odors, and they are practically the same ones that were used a hundred years ago. There are just over a hundred of them, whereas in perfumery we use thousands of scents. Children's responses to odors are always extraordinary. Another experiment that we did with 3-to-5-year-olds was to prepare colored cards where each color corresponded to an odor, for example, the color orange corresponded to the essence of orange, yellow to lemon, violet to lavender, and so on for a total of ten different colors and essences. The reactions were very strong both emotionally and in terms of how well the kids remembered the different odors and colors.

CTC: My interest in the olfactory universe and odors also started with color and a non-traditional approach to design. In my vision of the osmic dimension, odor is inseparable from the medium that is a vehicle for it; air assumes an indispensable role and the odor thus becomes an environmental characteristic. When I started to get into these areas I was wondering a lot about the nature of materials, which at that time interested me in all their facets: chromatic, tactile, olfactory. The immanent aspect, that is, the fact that an odor is associated with a substance became more important than exploring the syntax of the fragrances. I have always been interested in associating a perception with something objectifiable: the more a phenomenon is immaterial, the more strangely I feel the need for it to be connected to an objective medium. This is probably one of the differences between those who work with the emotional reality of things that have their own odor and those who work creating scent-

ed visions, pure perceptions. This approach derives perhaps from my industrial design background. Seeking to bring an emotional dimension to the world of automobiles, electronics, and chemistry, I started with the dimension of color. At the end of the seventies the advent of color sparked a great revolution in design history that needed planning because it required big investments. Today I see something similar happening in the osmic and gustatory worlds, extraordinarily well represented in the new enological culture. New generations are dedicating themselves to the development of the perception of very subtle and subjective aspects. This phenomenon highlights the new centrality of the subjective experience, and this marks a historic turning point.

LV: Drawing a parallel between the industrial world and that of colors, look at what has happened in the area of fragrance regarding the distinction between natural and synthetic. "Natural" in the biological sense regards something that is born and that dies, something that can be said to "live", that undergoes a biological growth process, such as a flower or a plant. However, "natural" in the sense of "belonging to the world of nature" is a very different concept. Here, even petroleum is natural, but it is not something that can grow or undergoes any sort of biological process of development. It is like a rock or a mineral. Now, as far as the concept of synthesis or "synthetic" goes, in relation to aromatic materials, the term can be applied to two different types of substances that have the same name. For example, linalool, the principal constituent of essential oil of lavender, can be obtained (isolated) from lavender oil or else synthesized from pinene and methyl-heptenone. In either case it is called "synthetic", while the "true" synthetic products are actually obtained from raw materials that are available in large quantities and at a low price, like, for example, petroleum, coal, and their derivatives. A common belief we often hear is that natural raw materials cost more than their synthetic counterparts. But there are natural materials such as oranges or pine trees that cost much less that many synthesized substances. To take a simple example, the main constituent in the smell of freshly cut grass, an alcohol called cis-3-hexanol, costs much more than a lot of natural essences. The natural ingredients have the charm of being associated with the earth, with

nature, with the changing of the seasons, and of never being the same from one time to the next. So the issue of whether an aromatic substances is natural or not is both technical and aesthetic. At the same time, when I think of what we have managed to obtain through analyzing the constituents of natural materials and synthesizing them I would not consider giving that up for a minute. You have to understand that not only would we not have been able to recompose the fragrances of many well loved or famous plants or flowers such as grass, lily of the valley, honeysuckle, lilac, gardenia, magnolia, and many others, but the quantity of different olfactory notes available to perfumers would also be very limited. In the letters and exchanges among perfumers in the late 1800s and early 1900s you understand that their main problem was the limited "alphabet" of odors at their disposal with just over a hundred almost completely natural ingredients at the end of the Nineteenth century.

CTC: I recognize a parallel with the world of new materials here. In design, the use of any material that imitates another is not appreciated. It is always better to choose the original. Hence, everything that is made synthetically just to cost less is generally considered a commercial expedient. Yet, more or less the same thing happened when we went from artificial materials to synthetic materials, for example from Bakelite to plastics. In this case the interest was purely technological. The designers were the first to use plastic materials for their own autonomous qualities. Originally the new materials were imitative, substitutes, ersatz; now it's no longer the case. There is still a lot of interest in synthetic materials. When a synthetic product – whether it falls into the category of perfumes or materials – is an imitation, it is generally crude, simple, not very complex. However, when it does not exist just to be a substitute for something else then amazing things are created. I think of the colors created with alizarin. Its synthesis led to color effects that had never been seen before. It was extraordinary, a great innovation.

LV: Synthetic substances principally represent the availability of ingredients for creating different nuances in a composition, in any kind of perfume base. They are generally not used as finished products; they are "ingredients" for the composition, not the composition itself.

CTC: But aren't there new synthetic products that don't resemble anything we know?

LV: In special synthesis processes under certain conditions and using special organic synthesis reactors we can obtain substances that do not exist in nature.

CTC: These are the areas that should be valorized, where it is worthwhile investing. Think for example of the pigments that didn't exist naturally but that then turned out to have extraordinary qualities.

LV: Synthetic substances that do not exist naturally are used along with special compounds to obtain "special effects", to add something new, something undecipherable and special to a given fragrance, not to imitate or reproduce something that already exists in nature.

CTC: Celluloid was a true imitation (a true surrogate) which was going well in Italy at the time when combs were made of horn. However, in the material culture world, new substances were well received and used rather intensively. I seem to understand, on the other hand, that the seductive aim of perfumes in the world of fragrances somewhat inhibits the potential for innovation. Whereas a color can in some way stir emotions or be seductive, or else be dynamic or basic, perfumes seem to be so strongly tied to the emotional and seductive sphere that there is little room for innovation. I wonder if fragrances could be produced that, even if they are not pleasant, could become iconic in a new way.

LV: It would be interesting to design odors as signals, as "signs", familiar or new odors that can distance themselves, where indicated, from pleasure and seduction. They would be "semaphore" odors, as it were, and also have other functions without forgetting the need to renew or enhance the fragrance itself. "Pleasure" in the world of odors is now strongly linked to recognizability, hence to memory, to the database of odors we have in our heads – but not exclusively.

CTC: Is that because the osmic world is so strongly associated with certain spheres of emotions that it is overly subjective?

LV: Our tastes are inevitably personal. What we like or dislike depends greatly – beyond the hereditary component that is so hard to determine – on our experience with odors in the first years of our life. An odor associated with good experiences is "memorized" as being good and likewise for bad odors. Then there are odors, such as those of various toxic substances or substances that are harmful to our olfactory apparatus, such as ammonia, that may be considered – in their pure state – as being almost universally negative. But everything in the world of odors depends on the degree and the context. A given substance in its pure form may be repulsive, whereas if it is diluted a hundred times and combined with other substances it may seem extremely nice. As for substances that are truly unknown and "unlike" any others existing in nature, perhaps it would be timely to empirically evaluate people's reactions to them in different proportions.

CTC: I once smelled an odor I had never smelled before. I was in a meat market in Mexico. The market was roofed but open-sided. It was clear that it was not kept very clean. Suddenly I caught a whiff of this indescribable sweetish smell. I took off like a crazy man! It was a reaction triggered more by instinct than by memory.

LV: One of the main problems regarding a given environment that has yet to be completely resolved is not that of perfuming it but rather that of eliminating or changing its odor. It is not all that simple to permeate a space with a fragrance, especially if it is large or public. The issue of perfuming a space is crucial, and the problem of how to change the odor of the air in a space still remains substantially unresolved.

CTC: Here we introduce another chapter, which is one about absence. In design, under the influence of Japanese culture, the existence of an odor may be reevaluated and worked with also in terms of its absence. In the mid eighties I was invited by the Milan *Triennale* to an exhibition on habitation which included various designers and explored the themes of air, dust, and odors. My contribution had to do with the use of water, light, and gas in the house. The result was the *Camera Linda* [Clean Room]: a household storage room that was meant to take the place of cupboards and that used an electrical appliance/door that kept the room under slight pressure, eliminating any dust and odors from the air.

LV: It brings to mind Süskind's book *Perfume* when the protagonist has to leave the place of all odors, Paris, to go into an odor-free cave, a place completely lacking any odor.

CTC: We should work to bring the rationale of design into the world of odors. It would be an experience like the one that led to the Slow Food movement for food.

LV: I agree. There are not enough interdisciplinary explorations and also too little research into new uses for perfumes and new ways of applying them.

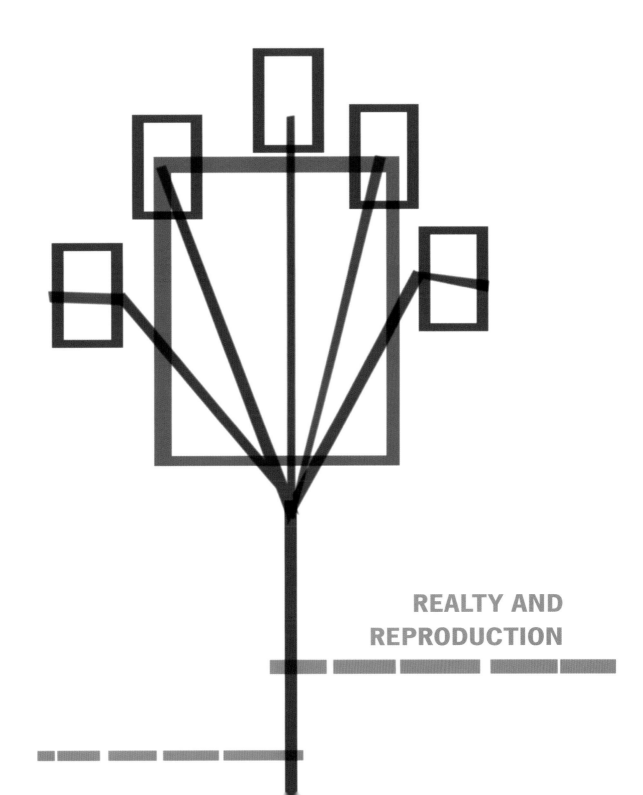

REALTY AND
REPRODUCTION

Confermare il reale

The increasing attention dedicated to the universe of odors in recent years has been driven partially by the possibilities offered by new technologies in defining architectural and urban spaces. Communications media, which have revolutionized geometrical and temporal relations, anthropological and proxemic relations, exhibit two different behaviors regarding the role of olfactory perception: on the one hand they seem to be solely concentrated on developing the technologies of the visible and audible and not particularly interested in what the nose knows; on the other they seem to be seeking its complicity to make immanent that which in reality is not immanent.

Olfaction, which is the sense of evanescence, illusion, the essence of absence, can now lend itself to becoming a measure of immanence, presence, reality. It can be thought of as a sort of synthesis of touch and taste, in which the rules of mechanics enter into play every bit as much as the rules of chemistry do. But the true current relevance of the sense of smell is captured in the words written by the anthropologist Franco La Cecla in an article published in the magazine *Domus* in the late 1980s: "[…] a geography of odors is only possible if we accept that they are fleeting. There are corners of jasmine without jasmine, façades of anise without anise, a carpet made of a weft of odors. The monotony of today's urban olfactory landscape is appalling. Automobiles and speed have killed nuance, variety, the very possibility of benefiting from the nature of olfaction. The passengers in boxes have their *Arbre Magique* that exorcises them from the city out there and the 'exhausted' fumes have reduced our nasal code to a constipated gibberish."

The cause and effect relationship between a material and its odor that has always existed appears to have fallen apart. They are no longer parties to an indivisible reciprocity. Odors are becoming more and more a decoration, an attachment added *ex post facto* in order to increase the emotional coefficient of the experience. The question of the relation between places and odors is currently caught between

Athena Temple, Delphi, Greece

two fundamentalist positions: the search for authenticity at all costs and thus the emphasis of the true nature of experiences, at times bordering on crude orthodoxy; and emotional marketing of the experience of place driven by a market that hungrily devours architecture in order to convert it, at all costs, into a memorable and extraordinary experience.

Vanilla and Vanillin

In order to get a better grasp on the relationship between a material and its true or presumed odor, it may be helpful to review what happened in the world of perfumes with the advent of synthetic substances.

The entrance into the market of synthesized molecules was initially associated with the need to respond to the scarcity or disappearance of certain raw materials, or simply their high cost. The early synthesized molecules emulated the original substances, they were copies and their names emphasized this imitative origin. One of the first synthesized substances was vanillin, produced by Wilhelm Haarmann, a young researcher from Holzminden, Germany during

the *Belle Époque*. And we are quite right in presuming it was a substitute for vanilla.

In that period the debate generally orbited around the shift from artisanal to industrial production methods and focused on the relation between the model and the copy. This is another one of those extraordinary contexts where architecture, design, and odors come together, as exemplified by the seminal debates on the relationship between the original and the copy in contemporary architecture between Hermann Muthesius and Henry Van de Velde, and between Adolf Loos and the secessionists.

Similarly in the world of colors and materials the new was legitimized only if obsequious to the original, only if it could evoke the memory of something that had already existed. No space was allotted the completely new; it was simply not admissible. Only the most daring designers, perfumers, and entrepreneurs began early on to see the "copies" as being more interesting than their models and hence as elements in their own right, unloosed from their generative matrices, and quite autonomously open to innovative compositions and intermixings. Vanillin, along with Bakelite, electric lighting, steel, and plywood later became ingredients that were more basic and versatile than "true" raw materials and ushered in new formulas and compositions. Brand new fragrances were created, substances that had no connection to any previously existing thing and were thus devoid of memory. The work of Aimé Guerlain was extraordinary in this regard. His creation, *Jicky*, in 1889, marked a break with traditional perfume. He did not seek to imitate nature, to reproduce well-known floral notes, but wanted to give birth to new emotions. His preference for chemistry over nature was audacious: *Jicky* was made with synthetic molecules and had a scent that made reference to nothing other than itself.

In this interplay of original and copy, of counterfeiting, we must mention an exhilarating ready-made by Marcel Duchamp, the *Belle Haleine: Eau de Voilette* (1921). He took a Rigaud perfume bottle and modified its color and label. The label is a true masterpiece: a photograph by Man Ray of Duchamp dressed as a woman.

Eating Aromas

The aroma industry is engaged in producing olfactory identities that orient the experience of a place, or that create new experiences. In certain ways this process negates the natural relation between places and odors, and sets out to explore new ones.

One of the earliest experiments was concocted by the Futurists in *Futurist Cooking*, where they described an *Exaggerated Meal* where the invitees "will not eat but will sate themselves with perfumes". The meal would take place in a villa "whose electrically-controlled window-doors, controlled by buttons at the invitees fingertips, give: the first, onto the mass of odors of the lake; the second, onto the mass of odors of the granary and its fruit bin; the third, onto the mass of odors of the sea and its haul of fish; the fourth, onto the warm greenhouse and its carousel of rare scented plants moving on rails. An August evening. The smells of the surrounding landscape are at the height of intensity, but they are kept outside of windows sealed like the locks in a canal. [...] Each guest will have a small hand-held fan with which to

The beauty of nature and its vast diversity lies in its simplicity.
by Isaac Sinclair

Colours are a good example of this. The entire spectrum of visible light can be illustrated in the variations of only three (RGB) or four (CMYK) colors. Every known colour can be created by mixing these fundamental elements in different proportions.

Nature, the eternal weaver always uses the same building blocks, where infinite creative possibilities are variations on a theme. Just as with colours, she comes up with very different smells by simply changing or tweaking the molecules proportions. Making seemingly vastly different smells by bringing out different aspects of their composition, by reducing or increasing an element in it. Today, the perfumers palette, called an organ, thanks to scientific breakthroughs over the last century or so, are largely composed of synthetic raw materials, molecules which, generally, are present in nature but have been isolated and produced synthetically. When we analyse one of natures masterpieces, the rose for example, what we have is a blend of olfactive molecules. The rose has around 300 "ingredients" which, in perfect harmony, come together to give us its signature scent. Of these ingredients however, only a few are of great importance. Less than twenty molecules are responsible for 90% of the way a rose smells. A spicy note, Eugenol, is the molecule responsible for making clove buds smell the way they do. When Eugenol is added to a rose accord, it becomes a Carnation accord. Sulfates play a part in many of natures most pungent "signatures" present in odors ranging from egg smells, to blackcurrant, and even cat piss. Nature has even blended sulphuric molecules with rose molecules, the surprising result being lychee!!! The molecule Linalool for example is an important constituent of bergamot oil, the citrus fruit which lends its odor to earl grey tea. Linalool is also what makes coriander oil and rosewood smell the way they do, and is also crucial in the chemical structure of orange blossom, tuberose, lily of the valley to list just a few. Benzyl Acetate has a wafting banana smell, so it's not surprising that it plays a major part in a bananas chemical make up. Amazingly, it is also an absolutely indispensable element of many more of nature's compositions. It is also the mellow airiness we perceive when we smell ylang ylang, gardenia, frangipani or jasmine. In Goethe's scientific writings he wisely observes that: "In an organic being, first the form as a whole strikes us, then its parts and their shape and combination."

When we take a closer look at nature, in any field, things which at first glance give us the impression of diversity, have in reality myriad forms but similar structures.

drive the enjoyed odor into the corner where it is sucked up by a powerful aspirator."

Several years ago the same provocations – or avant-gardism, who knows? – re-emerged in Spain: in his famous restaurant, *El Bulli*, the chef Ferran Adrià served his dishes among scents released from odor-filled balloons; Martí Guixé created a installation titled *Pharma Food* which involved a system of nourishment that worked via inhalation.

These are exercises in style, but they are also indicators of transformations underway. However, as Gianni De Martino writes in *Odori* [Odors]: "We can touch the wall and flood the room with light. We can turn the thermostat and create summer. We can surf the Internet and experience the delicious chaos of thousands of impalpable encounters and expanded consciousness. But we cannot give up the scent of the rose, of bread, or of love. We still inhabit the world of food and beverages, of feces and death."

Hallucinatory States and Metaspaces

We have already explored the capacity of odors to serve as a vehicle for visions, as a bridge to a celestial world beyond. It might also be interesting to consider the capacity of odors to be a vehicle for visions that do not go quite so far, but stop in mid-air, as it were. It's not a coincidence that "*vision-air*", the capacity to see in the air, means imagining something that is not present in the here and now.

Smoke, perfume, and drugs have always been hallucinatory media. Inhaling particular substances affects memory and spatial perception. They produce true olfactory hallucinations that are not to be taken lightly.

Set in the scenic and rugged landscape of Delphi, the Temple of Apollo was the most important religious site in ancient Greece. It was the site of the oracle Pythia, the medium chosen to give voice to Apollo. From the second millennium BC until the temple's destruction in 394 AD by the emperor Theodosius in the name of Christianity, Pythia's oracles influenced the political, military, civil, and institutional destinies of Hellas.

Pythia's prophecies were given on the seventh day of each month, except in winter, in an underground cell of the Temple. The oracle, seated on her tripod, hypnotized and inebriated by opiate fumes, held a sacred laurel twig and a woolen thread connected to the *omphalos*, the sacred stone that symbolized the center of the earth. Before pronouncing the prophecy, she chewed laurel leaves that induced a trance and then from behind a screen muttered obscure words that the temple priests would decipher. The ecstatic states were probably caused by vapors that issued from a cleft in the earth, by the leaves she chewed, and by the water from the Castalda fount. Callimachus in *The Olive and the Laurel* wrote: "The seat of Pythia is among the laurels. She sings of laurels and sleeps on laurels." Hence the hallucinations were caused by gaseous exhalations, but they were exhalations that shaped the imagination and foretold the future.

In Sumatra, healers (*batak*) use the resin *styrax* to enter into a state of trance, but it was also used to prepare the famous Javanese cigarettes of which Baudelaire sang of "the transport of the spirit and the senses".

Frazer relates in *The Golden Bough* that in the Hindu Kush the sibyl found her inspiration in the light of a fire of sacred cedar twigs, over which she bent her head wrapped in a cloak, breathing deeply. She soon would be seized by convulsions and fall unconscious to the ground. When she came to her senses she would pronounce the prophecy.

On the island of Madura off the north coast of Java, each spirit has its own medium through which to communicate with the living. In preparing to receive the spirit, the medium – usually a woman – sits with her head on a incense burner for a good while before being wracked by convulsions and falling to the ground.

Shamans in South America use tobacco as a means of entering the spirit world. They are not smokers, they are smoke eaters; they then blow it out to cure the sick, to drive off evil spirits, or to protect the harvest. In order to achieve a state of trance and to have visions that bring them into contact with the supernatural, they inhale mouthfuls of smoke from their pipes. The tobacco nourishes the spirits, who in turn protect the people in a mutualistic relationship.

And King Lear in Tudor England said: "Give me an ounce of civet, good apothecary, to sweeten my imagination."

But the most poetic victim of hallucinations and fantasies was Don Quixote, who exclaims upon seeing his love Dulcinea: "[…] these traitors were not content with changing and transforming my Dulcinea, but they transformed and changed her into a shape as mean and ill-favoured as that of the village girl yonder; and at the same time they robbed her of that which is such a peculiar property of ladies of distinction, that is to say, the sweet fragrance that comes of being always among perfumes and flowers. For I must tell thee, Sancho, that when I approached to put Dulcinea upon her hackney (as thou sayest it was, though to me it appeared a she-ass), she gave me a whiff of raw garlic that made my head reel, and poisoned my very heart."

Sometimes They Come Back Again: Odorama and Synesthesia

There are utopias that are never abandoned but tend to come back at regular intervals, perhaps somewhat as a provocation, and somewhat in the hope that now maybe the "right time" for success.

After the spread of home theater and Dolby Surround, it is only logical that the so-called odorama should reappear. Odorama was a means of projecting scented films in order to provide a more immersive experience for the spectator. Odorama was invented in the underground film world in the 1960s in the films of Yervant Gianikian and Angela Ricci Lucchi. It was further developed in the 1970s with the more well-known films of John Waters, such as *Polyester*, where the audience was given special scratch-and-sniff cards with numbers corresponding to different odors. On-screen cues would instruct the audience when to scratch each patch to have an olfactory accompaniment to the scene before their eyes. Odorama is back and around the world new methods are being implemented where instead of the scented cards there are special machines that generate puffs of wind and fog as well as scented breezes.

However the roots of stage machinery to com-

PIANODORANT: a Dream Instrument by Raphael Monzini

The words "organ", "notes", "harmony", are part of both a musician's and a perfumer's vocabulary.
In the olfactory world, an organ represents the perfumer's range of raw materials available for the creation of a perfume.
The notes classify and denote the various families of odors, such as "green notes", "floral notes", "spicy notes", or "woody notes".
Like the musician, the perfumer composes a story around a theme. The theme dominates the composition and determines the family of the perfume, while the secondary harmonies determine the subfamily.
Sound and scent already share terms and this complicity can be extended to the method of composition.
Hence the pianodorant.
It is a hybrid instrument, creating a symbiosis between the world of music and that of odors. The musician plays the composition through a synthesizer which sends the melody to the audio amplification section and also sends signals to a special hardware device (perfume amplifier) that decodes the notes. A special software transforms the audio signals into impulses that are sent to the "library of essences". These impulses are then represented olfactorily by the vaporization of the essences in our library. Thus the composer creates a composition which is both auditory and olfactory.
The pianodorant does not yet exist… but it won't be long.

Ferrari Wind Tunnel by Renzo Piano, Maranello, Italy (photo by S. Goldberg)

plement theatrical or cinematographic works with odors actually reach farther back. At the beginning of the Twentieth century an "odor organ" was built and played during recitals organized at the Central Hall of London. It was based on the same idea that odors can influence the emotional state of the audience.

In the 1970s, Superstudio developed a number of utopian projects which have since made regular reappearances in order to provoke a reaction, or perhaps simply for nostalgic reasons. One that was associated with odors was *Città 2000 t.*, a single, uninterrupted building composed of cubic cells arranged in a specific order. Each cell had two walls giving onto the outside made of an opaque material, permeable to air, rigid, but soft to the touch. One of the walls emitted three-dimensional images, sounds, and odors, while the opposite wall was occupied by a chair that adhered perfectly to and completely enveloped any human body. Each dwelling unit included apparatuses that were capable of meeting physiological, alimentary, excretory, and sexual needs. The membranous substance comprising the apparatus, when not in use, retracted along with its accessories to leave a blank wall. The ceiling was a single screen that received cerebral impulses and transmitted them to an electronic analyzer, which compared and balanced the desires of each in order to keep all citizens in a condition of equality.

Ubiquity

If we were to analyze human desires in depth, the true aspirations of humanity collectively and individually, we would discover that substantially there are not a great many of them, but rather a few primary desires that constitute matrices for many others.

One of the most deeply rooted desires is for ubiquity, i.e., the ability to be in different places, different contexts, different realities at the same time. Ubiquity carries with it the need for temporal synchronicity, for simultaneous experiences in different places. The ubiquity-simultaneity equation gives us the strongest impulses towards new communications technologies and others as well.

In *From A to B and Back Again* (1975), Andy

Warhol wrote that odor is really a means of transportation, that sight, hearing, touch, and taste are not powerful enough to transport you entirely to another spot. In this sense odors are extraordinary vehicles for traveling through both space and time. And they are also expedients for inhabiting different levels of existence simultaneously. An odor carries the mind to a place that is different from the one in which the body resides. Furthermore, the olfactory experience has the particular characteristic of bringing to life absent or even unreal places. However it produces very real emotions and concrete bodily reactions, just as memory does. It is a sort of voyeurism that allows certain olfactory behaviors to exercise a new rule over desire: the odor of a lover brings her closer than her photo does, as in Gustave Flaubert's deferred love for Louise Colet. In spatial terms it is a question of being in one place and breathing the odor of another so that the second one superimposes itself in some way on the first. It is the most immediate exercise suggested by odors, as Marcel Duchamp grasped in 1919 with *Air de Paris*, as is exemplified by perfumes that adopt the names of places, or as in Martí Guixé's recent creation *Montserrat Olor*, which evokes the local odor of the sacred mountain behind Barcelona.

Projects that seek to give concrete form to the ubiquity engendered by the sense of smell include those by the Korean artist Do-Ho Suh who creates ultralight, intangible, but real architecture. *Seoul Home* (1999) recreates the Korean home in a translucent textile (silk, organza) version that can be brought along on travels, a thin guest, a diaphanous architecture in the homes-away-from-home where it may abide.

Hyperventilation

The reproduction of the wind and its mechanical, thermal, and olfactory qualities is the focus of certain architectural experiments and works. This is nothing new if we think of the *fumarole* on the island of Pantelleria designed to best exploit the volcano's inner air, and a number of significant works of bio-climatic architecture. Nevertheless, recent progress in flow management has led to the development of particular-

Symbiotic Fragrance and the Rise of Meta-Humanity
di David Bychkov

1966: The US Air Force successfully collects human emotional data in flight by spraying uniform liners and cargo plane cockpits with inhalable biosensors that transmit data from the pilot's mouth, nose and lungs.

1996: IBM researchers announce the invention of PAN, Personal Area Networks, by which data could be temporarily stored and conducted across the surface of the skin. Thanks to PAN, business cards, video and other media can be transferred by handshake or kiss at ten megabytes per second.

2006: Bose researchers create ultra-sensitive radios that enable consumers to listen in to electrodermal changes stimulated by subconscious emotional responses to fragrance ingredients, including food aromatics. It is now imaginable to listen in to every phase of the digestive process in surround sound.

2016: Engineers at the US defense contractor Exmovere LLC develop fragrance ingredients that respond to mineral compositions in human sweat and change their molecular structure according to electrodermal changes associated with pain, pleasure or fear. The US Army sprays enemy detainee holding cells with fragrance chemicals that stimulate homosexual desire.

2017: The US Marine Corps sprays its warriors before battle with fragrance that stimulates bloodlust. That same year, Russian teenagers synthesize bloodlust fragrance from designs found on the internet and pump it through air conditioning vents at Moscow State University. Ten librarians are found dead with their chests gored by human teeth marks.

2018: US President Alan Keyes dies from cardiac arrest after his air conditioning operating system was attacked by a Trojan horse virus that switched it from Arctic Flower to Carbon Monoxide Garage fragrance. The Secret Service agent assigned to listen in to President Keyes' emotional states on his radio was asleep at his post.

2019: Keyes' successor, President Laura Ingraham, announces a new climate control measure whereby the entire country will be sealed in an air conditioned vacuum-locked artificial atmosphere. Congress approves a constitutional amendment that gives the President complete control over the Federal Thermostat, while guaranteeing individual States the right to choose air scent concentrations.

2020: The Micheline Guide now only reviews restaurants that offer digital fragrance cancellation technology so that critics can better discriminate between the smell of their food and the air conditioning.

2021: HomeDepot.com and Asianbeavers.com are the top sites for fragrance ingredient download.

2022: Korean researchers create artificially intelligent fragrance capable of seeking its own pleasure when applied to human skin. The only sample of it was immediately formatted and flushed down the toilet. Later that year a young girl in Seoul reports being sexually molested in a public fountain by sewer rats reeking of sandalwood.

2023: Scientologists claim to have offended the ghost of L. Ron Hubbard by accidentally contaminating his archives with *Chanel No. 0101001010001*.

2024:South African water fountains, swimming pools and hospitals are routinely sprayed with Citrus McAfee Antivirus to build up better immunity to AIDS, which mutated into digital form by 2019 and became communicable through certain potable liquids in Africa and elsewhere.

2025: Every Indian call center is retrofitted with spray nozzles that mist down frustrated data entrants with ionized Diet Coke to ensure comfort and modulate vital signs.

2026: Exmovere offers consumers Symbio, a fragrance that endows the wearer with superhuman capabilities: photographic memory, invulnerability to pain, momentary bursts of incredible strength, and the ability to impersonate animals. Batman and Spiderman sightings are now routine.

2036: . . .

ly interesting new buildings. One of the earliest ones was Toyo Ito's Wind Tower in Yokohama, built in 1986, which converted wind speed and direction and the intensity of traffic sounds into electrical signals that dynamically illuminated the tower-like structure.

Steven Holl's Turbulence House in New Mexico, built in 2002, is a more recent work. The house has a solar-panel power system and a rainwater collection tank. Its form is conceived to look like the tip of an iceberg suggesting a much larger hidden mass below, and it has an open center through which the desert winds can blow.

The idea of wind as the grand sculptor is embodied in many works by Renzo Piano, from the air intakes at the top of the Centre Pompidou in Paris (1977) to the Kansai International Airport (1983) or the Jean Marie Tjibaou Cultural Center (1983) in New Caledonia. But what is perhaps his most iconic work in his exploration of the relationship with the power of wind is the Wind Tunnel in the Renzo Piano Building Workshop in Maranello.

With respect to its predecessors, such as the wind tunnel built by Gustav Eiffel in Auteuil in 1912, in Piano's Maranello work the giant turbine is not enclosed and hidden within large industrial blocks, but left in full view: a sort of huge 70x80 meter engine. The huge tube seems to rest haphazardly on a slope, a design feature which provides dual access to the test room. The models to be tested, up to a scale of 1:1, are placed in a high quality flow of air (in terms of turbulence, angularity, and uniformity) generated by a 2,200 kW fan 5 meters in diameter. A sort of treadmill under the car moves in synchrony with the wind speed to cancel out the edge effect between the vehicle and the ground.

Pneumatic and Inflatable

The ascensional power of hot air was one of humanity's great discoveries, allowing us to reach hitherto unattainable heights, to move swiftly, to "fly". It was discovered through an empirical process two thousand years ago in the desolate lands of southern Peru, as indicated by the huge geoglyphs, some of them ten or twenty kilometers long, in the Rio Nazca valley. It remained an ambition over time that drew in many scientists and inventors, as recounts Benvenuto Cellini regarding Leonardo da Vinci who conducted experiments on the banks of the Tiber with hot air flight, inflating the bladders of dead animals. But it was the Montgolfier brothers in the late 1700s who finally succeeded in filling huge balloons with hot air and lifting off from the ground.

Using air as a structural element is possible in structures such as gasometers with their metal frame and internal bladder that inflated or deflated to accommodate the gas. A project along these lines is the work of the group of young designers known as the Breathing Design Team for the Nam June Paik Museum in Korea in 2004. Conceived as an artificial lung, it was designed for a number of functions including that of circulating air inside the building. The outer layer is a membrane connected to pistons that distribute the load uniformly over the entire mobile wall. Everything is controlled via a series of devices such as video cameras, microphones, photocells, and sensors for humidity, wind, and smog that provide data to the central computer program which then regulates the behavior of the building. Bioclimatic control is achieved by the cyclical inflation of the external skin, which, like a lung opens a valve to let air in at the moment of maximum expansion, and then lets it out again as it collapses.

Pneumatic or inflatable structures have become popular because they resolve a number of problems of contemporary architecture regarding temporariness and large dimensions. It was the ambition to achieve the perfection embodied by the spherical form and the lightness of a dome that led to what we now call inflatable architecture. This is well exemplified in works such as the Allianz Arena in Munich by Jaques Herzog and Pierre de Meuron for the 2006 soccer World Cup. The structure comprises an envelope formed of 3,000 pillow-shaped panels in ETFE. The panels on top are transparent to let in light, including UV rays to keep the grass healthy. The façade panels are translucent and have recessed spotlights that change color depending on which team is playing. Each panel can be inflated with dehumidified air at varying pressures to withstand the loads caused by wind or snow.

Desert Seal is a prototype designed by Andreas Vogler and Arturo Vittori which was presented at the *Safe* exhibition in 2005 at the New York MoMA. It is a sort of tent whose form and section were designed for sleeping out in the desert. It resolves the problems of protection both from the sun and the wind, which is of critical importance in preventing dehydration in hot and dry climes. Its L-shaped section provides for optimal air management: during the day the cool air at ground level is driven into the tent through an opening at the top; at night the opening captures warm air. This opening, which functions as a natural ventilation system, is used in traditional Islamic architecture for air circulation. It is noteworthy that this micro-architecture also performs optimally in the opposite conditions, i.e., in arctic areas. The tent accommodates one person either lying down or standing up.

Technology
by Erminia
De Luca, 2005

Bibliography

D. Ackerman, *Storia naturale dei sensi*, Frassinelli, Como 1992

P. Antonelli, *Safe. Design Takes on Risk*, MoMA, New York 2005

Arabian Nights, translation Andrew Lang, 1898

P. Ariés, G. Duby, *La vita privata*, Laterza, Bari 1988

P. Atkins, *Atkins' Molecules*, Cambridge University Press, Cambridge 2003

A. Aymonino, V. P. Mosco, *Spazi pubblici contemporanei. Architettura a volume zero*, Skira, Milan 2006

P. Ball, *Colore. Una biografia*, BUR, Milan 2001

R. Banham, *Ambiente e tecnica nell'architettura moderna*, Laterza, Bari 1978

A. Barbara, *Storie di architettura attraverso i sensi*, Bruno Mondadori, Milan 2000

R. Barbaras, *La percezione. Saggio sul sensibile*, Mimesis, Milan 2002

G. Bassanini (ed.), *Architetture del quotidiano*, Liguori, Naples 1995

G. Bassanini, *Tracce silenziose dell'abitare*, Liguori, Naples 1990

C. Baudelaire, *Fleurs du Mal, Petit Poems en Prose*, Gallimard, Paris 1999

M. Belpoliti, *Crolli*, Einaudi, Turin 2005

L. Benevolo, *Storia dell'architettura moderna*, Laterza, Bari 1985

A. Brillat-Savarin, *Fisiologia del gusto*, BUR, Milan 1985

I. Calvino, *Under the Jaguar Sun*, Harcourt Brace & Company, Orlando 1988

P. Camporesi, *La miniera del mondo*, Il Saggiatore-Mondadori, Milan 1990

P. Camporesi, *I balsami di Venere*, Garzanti, Milan 1989

P. Camporesi, *Il governo del corpo*, Garzanti, Milan 1995

P. Camporesi, *La carne impassibile*, Garzanti, Milan 1994

P. Camporesi, *Le officine dei sensi*, Garzanti, Milan 1991

Catullus, translated by Rudy Negenborn

Song of Solomon, King James Bible

L. F. Céline, *Viaggio al termine della notte*, Corbaccio, Milan 2005

Centre Pompidou, *Architectures non standard*, Catalogue Exposition, Éditions du Centre Pompidou, Paris 2003

G. Ceronetti, *Il silenzio del corpo*, Adelphi, Milan 1979

B. Chandler, *L'imperatore del profumo*, Rizzoli, Milan 2005

Conan Doyle, Sir Arthur, *The Hound of the Baskervilles*

E. B. Condillac, *Trattato delle sensazioni*, Laterza, Bari 1977

A. Corbin, *Storia sociale degli odori*, Paravia Bruno Mondadori, Milan 2005

H. Cortés, *La Conquista del Messico*, Istituto Geografico De Agostini, Novara 1967

W. J. R. Curtis, *L'architettura moderna del Novecento*, Bruno Mondadori, Milan 1999

A. De Angelis, *Gaetano Pesce. The Scent of Material*, Modo, Milan 2005

N. De Barry, M. Turonnet, G. Vindry, *Piccola Enciclopedia del profumo*, Rizzoli, Milan 2004

E. De Luca, *I colpi dei sensi*, Fahrenheit 451, Rome 1993

G. De Martino, *Odori*, Apogeo, Milan 1997 [translation Skira]

J.-G. Décosterd, P. Rahm, *Architettura Fisiologica*, Birkhäuser, Basel 2002

J.-G. Décosterd, P. Rahm, *Distorsions*, HYX, Orleans, 2004

D. DeFoe, *Journal of the Plague Year*, 1722

M. Detienne, *Dioniso e la pantera profumata*, Laterza, Bari 1980

Ph. Dick, *Ubik*, Vintage Books, New York 1991

T. Doi, *Anatomia della dipendenza*, Cortina, Milan 1991

G. H. Dodd, S. Van Toller, *Fragranze. Psicologia e biologia del profumo*, Aporie, Rome 1998

G. Duff, *Il mio profumo*, Garzanti, Milan 1995

U. Eco, *La struttura assente*, Bompiani, Milan 1983

N. Elias, *La civiltà delle buone maniere*, il Mulino, Bologna 1982

T. Engen, *The Perception of Odors*, Academic Press, New York 1982

I. Faré (ed.), *Il discorso dei luoghi*, Liguori, Naples 1992

S. Ferino-Pagden (ed.), *Immagini del sentire. I cinque sensi nell'arte*, Leonardo Arte, Cremona 1996

E. Fiorani, *Leggere i materiali*, Lupetti, Milan 2000

M. Foucault, *Le parole e le cose*, Rizzoli, Milan 1967

M. Ghyka, *The Geometry of Art and Life*, Dover Publications, New York 1977

N. Gogol, *The Nose* from *St. Petersburg Stories*

E. H. Gombrich, *Il senso dell'ordine*, Einaudi, Turin 1984

J. Gontier, J. C. Ellena, *Mémoires du Parfum*, Équinoxe, Barbentane 2003

E. Grazioli, *La polvere nell'arte*, Bruno Mondadori, Milan 2004

N. Grimal, *Storia dell'Antico Egitto*, RC, Milan 2004

E. Guidoni, *Architettura primitiva*, Electa, Milan 1979

A. Gusman, *Antropologia dell'olfatto*, Laterza, Rome-Bari 2004

R. Guy, *Le Sens du Parfum. I sensi e l'essenza del profumo*, Franco Angeli, Milan 2003

L. Gwiazdzinski, *La Ville 24 hours sur 24*, Éditions de l'Aube, Paris 2003 [translation Skira]

E. T. Hall, *La dimensione nascosta*, Bompiani, Milan 1966

M. Harris, *Buona da mangiare*, Einaudi, Turin 1990

J. D. Hoag, *Architettura Islamica*, Electa, Milan 1973

S. Holl, *Parallax*. Princeton Architectural Press, New York 2000

R. P. Hupp, *I sigari*, L'ippocampo, Genoa 2004

J.-K. Huysmans, *Controcorrente*, Garzanti, Milan 1975

L. Impelluso, *La natura e i suoi simboli*, Electa, Milan 2004

C. Jencks, G. Baird, *Il significato in architettura*, Dedalo Libri, Bari 1974

C. Jencks, K. Kropf, (ed.), *Theories and manifestoes of contemporary architecture*, Academy, Chirchester 1997

P. Jodidio, *Building a new millennium*, Taschen, Cologne 2000

T. Kalopissis, *La livre des maisons du monde*, Gallimard, Paris 1986

D. Laporte, *Storia delle merda,* Multipla Edizioni, 1979

R. Lawlor, *Sacred Geometry*, Thames and Hudson, London 1992

J. Lenoir, *Alla ricerca del naso perduto,* Jean Lenoir, 2000

D. Lenti Boero, M.Puntellini, *Oltre le parole*, Quattroventi, Urbino 2000

A. Leroi-Gourhan, *Il gesto e la parola*, Einaudi, Turin 1977

M. Mairani, *Le navi del cielo*, Ambrosino, Milan 1993

F. T. Marinetti, Fillìa, *La cucina futurista,* Christian Marinotti, Milan 1998 [translation Skira]

G. Marrone (ed.), *Sensi e discorso*, Progetto Leonardo, Bologna 1995

D. Martellotti, *Architettura dei sensi*, Mancosu, Rome 2004

P. Matvejević, *Mediterraneo*, Garzanti, Milan 1991

M. McLuhan, *Understanding Media*, Mc-Graw Hill, New York 1964

M. McLuhan, *Gli strumenti del comunicare,* Net, 2002

W. I. Miller, *Anatomia del disgusto*, McGraw-Hill, Milan 1998

T. Mori (ed.), *Immateriale/Ultramateriale*, Postmedia Books, Milan 2004

I. Naegele, R. Baur, *Scents of the city*, Lars Muller Publishers, Baden 2004

T. Nathan, *Principi di etnopsicoanalisi*, Bollati Boringhieri, Turin 1996

E. Norbert, , *La civiltà delle buone maniere*, il Mulino, Bologna 1982

P. Nuttgens, *The Story of Architecture*, Phaidon, London 1997

H. U. Obrist, *Interviste. Volume primo*, Charta e Edizioni Pittimmagine Discovery, Milan 2003

O.M.A., R. Koolhaas, B. Mau, *S,M,L,XL*, 010 Publishers, Rotterdam 1995

P. P. Pasolini, *Odore dell'India*, Guanda, Milan 2005

O. Pastorelli, *Il profumo dello spazio*, Franco Angeli, Milan 2003

O. Pastorelli, S. Levi, *Leggere il profumo*, Franco Angeli, Milan 2005

L. Patetta, *Storia dell'architettura. Antologia critica*, Etas, Milan 1989

C. Pergola, *La città dei sensi*, Alinea, Florence 1997

R. Pierantoni, *Verità a bassissima definizione*, Einaudi, Turin 1998

L. Pignotti, *I sensi delle arti*, Dedalo, Bari 1993

Plutarch, *Il tempo di Giulio Cesare*, Istituto Geografico de Agostini, Novara 1966

Plutarch, *Antony*, translated by John Dryden

M. Polo, *Il Milione*, Istituto Geografico De Agostini, Novara 1966

M. Proust, *Alla ricerca del tempo perduto,* Mondadori, Milan 1998

D. Riccò, *Sinestesie per il design*, Etas, Milan 1999

A. Roob, *Alchimia & Mistica*, Taschen, Cologne 2003

T. Rosebury, *Igiene e pregiudizio*, Garzanti, Milan 1970

G. Rosetti, *Notandissimi Secreti de l'arte profumatoria*, Neri Pozza, Vicenza 1973

M. Rossi, *Il libro del profumo*, TEA, Milan 2004 [translation Skira]

P. Rovesti, *Alla ricerca dei profumi perduti*, Marsilio, Padua 1980

O. Sacks, *The Man Who Mistook His Wife for a Hat*, Touchstone, New York 1998

C. Schittich, *Building Skins*, Birkhäuser Edition Detail, Basel 2001

Shigeru Ban, Editorial Gustavo Gili, Barcelona 1997

D. M. Stoddart, *La scimmia profumata*, CIC, Rome 2000

Studio Azzurro, *Mediterraneo. Meditazioni*, Silvana Editoriale, Milan 2002

P. Süskind, *Perfume*, Knopf, New York 1986

M. Tafuri, F. Dal Co, *Architettura contemporanea*, Electa, Milan 1979

J. Tanizaki, *In Praise of Shadows*, Leete's Island Books, New Haven 1977

Teofrasto, *De Odoribus*

G. Teyssot (ed.), *Il progetto domestico*, Electa, Milan 1986

P. Verlaine, *Trilogia erotica*, Edicart, Milan 1991

Vitruvius, *De Architectura*, Studio Tesi, Pordenone 1990

P. Vroon, *Il seduttore segreto. Psicologia dell'olfatto*, Editori Riuniti, Rome 2003

O. Wilde, *Picture of Dorian Gray*

M. Zardini, *Sense of the City. Un alternative approach to urbanism*, Canadian Centre for Architecture, Lars Müller Publishers, Montréal 2006

E. Zola, *Ventre di Parigi,* Gallimard, Paris 2002

P. Zumthor, *Atmosphere*, Paths to Architecture, Cologne 2003

Contributors

DAVID BYCHKOV

A New York native, David Bychkov was Professor of Holographic Cinema and Psychophysiology, and Director of the Laboratory of Psychophysiology, where he managed EEG and skin conductance studies.

Founder of Exmovere LLC, an American small business dedicated to creating wearable biosensors, reliable emotion detection technologies and better human performance training systems. His contribution for the book is a projection of the future of symbiotic fragrances on the next humanity.

ERMINIA DE LUCA

Photographer and artist, Erminia's artistic quest focuses mainly on the black and white. She was one of the artists chosen by the European and Mediterranean Biennial Exhibition of Young Artists in Rome (1999). She has taken part in numerous artistic and photographic exhibitions. The most famous of her personal exhibitions was one entitled "25 ASA".

FABRIZIO GALLANTI

Architect and cofounder of the A12 group (Milan/Genoa), he lives and works in Santiago, Chile, where he teaches at the Pontificia Universidad Católica. He writes articles for international magazines and has won a number of architectural design competitions. Over the past three years he has sent images of Chilean

architecture on a daily basis via email to all his friends. A fragrant selection of these images is contained in this book.

SARA MANAZZA

Sara has been involved in sensory and strategic design for years. She currently conducts research in design and fashion trends and studies the contribution of our senses in aesthetic philosophy. Her contribution to this book is a short discussion of the theory of humors.

NANCY MARTIN

Nancy Martin is a professional textile designer and educator who uses a sensory approach to researching developing and communicating product design. She spent all her life travelling around the world. Her writing for the book is the shortest trip she did recently in a Chinese shop at the corner of the town she used to live.

RAPHAEL MONZINI

Expert in sound, video, graphics, and music, Raphael is a creative designer in the audio-visual realm. In his restless development and research he has become familiar with the realm of odors which he seeks to capture and translate in his professional work. His contribution to this book is the description of a possible invention to combine sounds and odors.

NICOLA POZZANI

A young researcher in perfumes, Nicola is involved in creative design and research, for Italian and international perfume companies. His contribution to this book is a brief piece on the osmic interweave between the city of Parma and its violet.

CAROLINA RAPETTI
Copyrighter, researcher in fashion and design, inventor of children's fables, Carolina lives in London and works in Milan, where she deals with olfactory design and education. Her personal quest involves an exploration of the various sensory approaches to creativity. Her contribution to this book is a summary of the meaning of absence and essence as the matrix for any olfactory experience.

ROMINA SAVI
After receiving her degree in Business Administration, Romina concentrated on studying taste and scents in her professional career. In January 2005 she became an advertising journalist and manages event organization and publicity for one of Italy's most renowned restaurants. Her contribution to his book is an olfactory recipe that includes sensory inputs among its ingredients.

LETIZIA SCHMID
Letizia Schmid wrote her PhD thesis on the experience of pleasure, frustration and the body in the reading process at King's College London. He teaches and writes on world literature and questions of identity in the New York City's area. Her contribution for the book is a writing about Derrida's thoughts on the essence of the roses.

ISAAC SINCLAIR
Growing up in New Zealand's Waitakere Ranges, Isaac Sinclair had the privilege to be exposed to a rich variety of "smells" and now resides in Paris where he is an up and coming perfumer. His contributions for the book is a landing in the world of scents.

Index

Aalto, A., 178
Ackermann, D., 148
Adrià, F., 203
Al Pacino, 123
Alexander the Great, 148
Alhambra Gardens (Granada), 56
Ali, M., Cassius Clay, 146
Amalfi 82
Ambasz, E., 39
Amsterdam, 155, Zaanse windmills, 161
Ando, T., 47
Antioch, 85
Anwar, G., 123
Arensberg, W., 81
Aristotle, 143
Asplund, G., 178
Assam, 69
Auda, D., 82
Augé, M., 91
Auschwitz, 40
Axel, R., 15
Azari, F., 32

Babylon, Hanging Gardens, 56
Bach, J.S., 58
Bagdad, 59
Bahia, Bahia House, 117
Bali, Denpasar market, 89
Balkenende, J.P., 166
Baltic sea, 85
Ban, S., 118, 149
Bangkok, *13*
Barbara, A. *13, 181*
Barcelona, 209
Baricco, A., 76
Barragán, L., 145, 165
Barthes, R., 29
Basque Country, *62*

Bataille, G., 153
Baudelaire, C., 119, 204
Bear run, 183, falling water, 183
Beecher, C., 62
Beecher, H., 62
Bejing, Water Cube, 147
Belpoliti, M., 40
Berlin Wall, 40, Danish Embassy, 185
Berlusconi, S., 166
Billot, 115
Bjork, 35
Blaisse, P., 57, 118, 157, 161, 185
Boelens, H., 117
Borromini, L., 119
Boulder, College of Engineering
    University of Colorado, 186
Boullée, E.-L., 79
Branzi, A., 150
Brazil, Minas Gerais, 69
Bregenz, Kunsthaus, 179
British Columbia, 135
Buck, L., 15
Bulgari, 97
Burkina-Faso, 122
Bush, G., 166

Cairo, 69
Calder, A., 109
Callimachus, 204
Calvino, I., 93, 111, 142
Cambridge (Ma), 123, Splice Garden 59,
    Whitehead Institute 59
Cameroon, 122
Cappadocia, 122
Caravaggio, Michelangelo Merisi known
    as, 36
Casanova, G., 150
Casillas, A, 144
Catullus, G.V., 150
Cellini, B., 213
Cézanne, P., 109
Chanel, C., 84

Chernobyl, 40
Chicago, Illinois Institute of Technology,
    185, World's Columbian Exposition,
    62, World's Fair, 65
China, 24, 147
Christie, A., 68
Cleopatra, 148
Clermont-Ferrand, Vulcania, 60, 61
Colet, L., 209
Cologne, 82, Werkbund Exposition,
    Glass Pavillion, 54
Columbus, C., 67, 86
Corinth, 41, 85
Cornwall, Eden Project, 77
Cortés, H., 32
Costantinople, 85
Coty, F., 54
Crete, Palace of Knossos, 181
Cretzer, J.P., 156
Cuba, 67, 68
Curtis, W.J.-R., 120

D'Arcet, J., 30, 174
d'Este, I., 148
Dalí, S., 74
Damascus, 57, 59
Dante Alighieri, 60
Davidoff, Z., 68
de Beauharnais, J., 173
De Filippo, E., 68
de la Sota, A., 146
de Luca, E. 41
De Luca, E., *42, 70, 94, 130, 158, 186,*
    214
De Maria, W., 74
De Martino, G., 140, 203
de Meuron, P., 213
de Sade, Marquis, 156
de' Medici, Caterina, 148
de' Medici, Cosimo, 189
Deaborn (Mi), Dymaxion House, 77,
    Henry Ford Museum, 77

Décosterd, J.-G., 13, 55, 56, 86, 94, 146
Defoe, D., 53
Delphi, Greece, Athena Temple, *198,*
    Temple of Apollo, 203
Derrida, J., 116
Detroit, Lafayette Park, 184
Devalle, G., 152
Di Pierantonio, G., 55
Diaz, N., *62*
Dick, Ph., 37
Diller, E., 133, 181
Diogenes, 172
Dodd, G. H. 21
Do-Ho, Suh, 209
Dryden, E., 54
Duchamp, M., 39, 81, 111, 201, 209
Dumas, R., 97
Duvall, R., 123

Egypt, 19, 64
Eiffel, G., 212
e-Khoury, R., 15
Elias, N., 172
Eliasson, O., 179
Ellena, C., 129
Ellena, H., 97
Ellena, J.-C., 97
Eno, B., 90
Erasmus of Rotterdam, 171, 172
Eritrea 64
Ethiopia, Nyangatom, *109*
Euphrates, 85

Farina, J.-A., 82
Faubourg 45
Flaubert, G., 209
Florence, 82, 135, Giardino dei
    Semplici, 11, 189, Officina
    Farmaceutica Santa Maria Novella, 24
Foremann, G., 146
Foucault, M., 18
France 48, 69, 85, 97, 162

Francis I of Austria, 45
Frank, A., 155
Franko B., 35
Frazer, J.G., 204
Frederick, C., 62
Freud, S., 29
Fromm, E., 31
Fuller Buckminster, R., 77

Galen Claudius, 26
Garnier, T., 174
Gateway Village, North Carolina, Wind
    Veil, 185
Gaudí, A., 120
Genet, J., 153
Geneva, 68, Expo 181
Genoa, *74*, 80, 82, 128
Germany, 200
Giacometti, A., 22
Gianikian, Y., 205
Gigon, A., 39
Giuxé, M., 203, 209
Goethe, J.W., 202
Gogol, N., 92
Goldberg, S., *206*
Gras, M., 110, 161
Grasse, 82, 85
Grazioli, E., 40
Great Britain, 69, 174
Greece, 106
Grimshaw, N., 77
Gucci, 45
Guerlain, A., 201
Guerlain, J., 129, 130
Guo-Qiang, C., 74, 76
Guyer, M., 39
Gwiazdzinski, L., 128, 129

Haarmann, W., 200
Hadid, Z., 74, 76
Hafner, G., *35*
Halifax, 141

Hallè, J. N., 173
Hannover, Expo Swiss pavilion, 158
Harar, 65
Haring, H., 144
Haussmann, G. E.,173
Heliogabalus, Marcus Aurelius
    Antoninus, 82
Hennig 115
Heraclites, 90
Hermès, 11, 45, 97, 98
Herzog, J., 213
Hindu Kush, 204
Ho-Chi-Min City 165
Holl, S., 91, 118, *174*, 179, 212
Holland, 11
Hollein, H., 61
Holmes, S., 115
Holzminden, 200
Homer, 106
Hondarribia, *62*
Huysmans, J.K., 32, 119

India, 24, 69, Khyougtha hill, 153
Indonesia, 38
Istanbul, 46, 69, 182
Italy, 135
Ito, T., 212

Japan, 84, 91, 179
Java, 204
Jeanneret, P., 184
Jerusalem, 59
Johnson, Ph., 149
Josephine Beauharnais, 84
Jura, 39

Kahn, N., 179, 185
Kansai, International Airport, 212
Kant, I., 143
Kaufmann, E., 183
Kinshasa, 146
Klimt, G., 54

Klinck T., 14
Korea, Nam June Paik Museum, 213
Kusolwong, S., *13*

La Cecla, S., 198
Lalique, R., 54
Lambot, J.-L., 99
Lang, H., 135
Lauder, E., 48
Le Corbusier, known as C. E. Jeanneret,
    47, 59, 124, 178, 183, 184
Leibniz, G., 109
Leonardo da Vinci, 213
Lille, Grand Palais, 185
Linnaeus, C., 115
London, 93, 147, 148 *155*, AA School,
    45, Central hall, 208, Crystal Palace,
    82, Heatrow Airport, 91, Zoo, 146
Loos, A., 54, 70, 200
Los Angeles, Barnsdall House, 183
Los Clubes (Mexico), 144
Lubeck, 144, Cowshed at Garkau, 144
Lubetkin, B., 146
Lucretius Caro, T., 114
Luis XV, of France, 82, 119
Luxor (Egypt), Temple, 21

Madrid, The Maravillas College
    Gymnasium, 146
Madura, 204
Maldives, 93
Malle, F., 45, 97
Man Ray, 201
Manzoni, P., 81
Maranello (Italy), Ferrari Wind Tunnel,
    206, 212, Renzo Piano Building
    Workshop, 212
Marco Polo, 86, 91
Marie Antoniette, 84
Marie Luise von Habsburg, 78
Marinetti, T.F., 31, 107
Mark Antony, 149

Marseilles, 171
Mattè-Trucco, G., 178
Matvejevic, P., 124
May, E., 62
McKimm, F., 123
McLuhan, M., 74, 81
Merleau-Ponty, M., 110
Metheney, P., 58
Michigan, Cranbook Institute of Science, Steam House, *174*, 179
Mies van der Rohe, L., 149, 184
Milan, 57, Triennale, 117
Miller, W. I., 153
Möbius known as Jean Giraud, 107
Mollino, C., 152
Montgolfier, 213
Monzini, R., *74*
Mori, T., 14
Moscow, Dubrovka Theater, 42, State University, 210
Müller, V., 80
Munari, B., 109
Munich, 128, Allianz Arena, 213
Muthesius, H., 200
Mycenae, 61

Nagel, C., 47
Nakagawa, Y., 57
Nakdong River, 38
Naples 60
Napoleon I, 84, 148
Napoleon III, 45
Narlai, Rajasthan, Shiva Altar, *53*
Nero, Lucius Domitius, 82
Neuchâtel, 134, Blur Building, 134
Neutra, R., 13, 178
New Caledonia, Jean Marie Tjibaou Cultural Center, 212,
New Guinea, 106
New Jersey, 133, 135
New Mexico, Turbulence House, 212
New Orleans, 37, 38

New York 48, 74, 128, 135, 148, 185, Broadway, Paramount Theater, 124, Chelsea, 133, Cooper Hewitt Museum, 185 Garbage Dump, *35*, Manhattan, 40, 133, 134, 148, 184, Meatpacking district, 11, 133, 134, MoMA, 111, 133, 214, Rose Center for Earth and Space, 179, Second Stage Theater, 185, Twin Towers, 40, West Village, 133, Whitney Museum of American Art, 111, World Trade Center, 40
Nietzsche, F., 46
Nieuwegein (Holland), penitentiary, 157
Nile, 85

Oak park, 183
Obrist, H. U., 184
Olbrich, J.-M., 120
Orwell, G., 153, 155
Osiris, 54

Palermo, San Giovanni degli Eremiti, *67*
Palm Springs 178
Palmyra, 85
Pantelleria, 209
Paracelsus, 93
Pardoe, J., 182
Paris 37, 45, 48, 81, 97, 84, 85, 128, 129, 135, 173, 194, 14th arrondissement, 45, Atelier Hermès, 11, 97, Barbès, 129, Bastille 156, Beistegui Apartment, 59, 183, Catacombs, 11, 45, Cemetery of the Innocents, 45, Centre Georges Pompidou, 45, 109, 212, Cité de refuge of the Salvation Army, 184, Exposition of Decorative Arts, 84, Foundation Cartier pour l'Art Contemporain, 56, 45, Insitut de France, 97, La Défense, 129, Metro, *150*, Musée d'Art Moderne, 94, Musée de l'Homme, *109*, Notre

Dame, 47, Père Lachaise Cemetery, *21*, World's Fair, 84
Parma, 78, 89, Museo del Profumo, 78, Museo Napoleonico, 78, palazzina Borsari 78
Pasteur, L., 170
Paxton, J., *82*
Peclet 174
Perliss, A. *21, 53, 120, 144, 150*
Perù 212
Pesce, G., 37, 117
Petra, 85
Pevsner, A., 107
Piano, R., 77, 212
Piotrowski, M., 93
Pisa, 82
Plano, Farnsworth house, 149
Plutarch, 149
Poincaré, H., 109
Polybius, 41
Porter, C., 89
Portoghesi, P., 119
Price, C., 146, 184
Proust, M., 122
Providence, Airport Terminal, 179

Rahm, Ph., 13, 45, 55, 56, 86, 94, 146
Rahmé, L., 128
Rajasthan, Bundi Palace, *120*
Reinhart, O., 39
Rhode Island, 179
Ricci Lucchi, A., 205
Rimmel, 115
Rio Nazca, 213
Robert, G., 115
Robinson, A., 109
Rodchenko, A., 109
Rome, Baths of Caracalla 182, Casa dei Filippini, 119, Cloaca Maxima, 30, Coliseum, 33, San Carlino, 119, Sant'Agnese, 119, Villa Medici Accadémie de France, 45

Rossi, M., 130
Rother, 152
Roucel, M., 45
Roudnitska, E., 119
Rovaniemi, 74, 76
Rufus, 150
Ruiz de Azúa, M., 80
Ruskin, J., 157
Russia, 24
Rykwert, J., 10

Sacks, O., 125
San Francisco Bay, Alcatraz Prison, *144*, 156, 157, Island of Alcatraz, 156
San Francisco, California Academy of Science, 77, Exploratorium, 179, New Langton Arts, 179
Santiago, 126
Saraceno, T., 80
Savinio, A., 128, 152
Savoye, France, villa 183
Scheenwind, K., 123
Scheerbart, P., 53
Schlemmer, O., 107
Schmid, R., 133
Schütte Lihotzky, M., 62
Schwaller, R. A. 21, 22
Schwartz, M., 59
Scofidio, R., 181
Seattle, 165, central library, 161
Seville, 68
Sheldrake, C., 47
Siberia, 147
Spiegelman, A., 40
Spielberg, S., 35
Staehle, W., 40
Sumatra, 38, 204
Süskind, P., 37, 60, 87, 128, 194
Swift, J., 153

Tanizaki, J., 30
Tarantino, Q., 35

Tasso, T., 60
Taut, B., 53, 54
Tenochtitlan 32
Thailand, 38
Theodosius, 204
Tibet, 147
Tigris, 85
Tivoli, Hadrian's Villa, 181
Tokyo, 48, Curtain Wall, House, 149, space Hermes, 57
Tredgold, Th., 174
Trent, 172
Trini Castelli, C., 93, 123, 189
Tschumi, B., 32, 109
Turin, Lingotto, 178
Turner, J. M. W., 157

United States, 35, 36, 91

Vai, S., 58
Valéry, P., 128
Vals, Thermal Bath, *181*, 182
Van Cleef & Arpels, 97
Van de Velde, H., 120, 200
Van Toller, S., 21
Venice, 69, 82, 128, Biennale, 45, Fondazione Bevilacqua La Masa, 55, Swiss Pavilion, 86
Vienna Cafe Museum, 70, Secession Building, 120
Viet Nam, 143
Villoresi, L., 189
Vitruvius Pollio, 170, 184
Vittori, A., 214
Vogler, A., 214
von Trier, L., 35
Voytzis, C., 97

Warhol, A., 35, 124, 208, 209
Waters, J., 205
Westwood, V., 161
Wilde, O., 147

Winterthur, Swiss Science Center, Technorama Facade, 185
Wisconsin, 134, Johnson's Wax Building, 134
Wright, F.L., 61, 183

Yamasaki, M., 41
Yellow River, 85
Yoh, S., 179
Yokohama, Wind Tower, 212

Zaansdrake, 11
Zaire, 146
Zappa, F., 58
Zola, É. 119
Zumthor, P., 157, 179, *181*, 182
Zurich, Switching Box, 39